Tattletales

And
Other Southern Shenanigans

By

Lee St. John

Lee St. John (signature)

"Teachers will love *Teacher Tattletales and other Southern Shenanigans,* as Lee recalls the best and the worst of students, parents, faculty, and even herself. Lee ventures outside the classroom as she tattles on the challenges of raising two rascally boys, especially one, who as a child, once loved to dress-up as super heroes. In 'Going AWOL,' she threatens this elementary aged son with military school. It backfires, as her son said he'd love to have the opportunity to wear uniforms and handle weapons. In 'Lies Our Mothers Told Us' the hilarious list includes one mom who confided 'When the ice cream truck plays the music, that means it's out of ice cream' and another who gave her kids a department store threat, 'Every time you touch something in this store, a kitten dies.'

The second half of her book is a pure delight of shenanigans as she parodies, well, classroom curriculum. The book is a wonderful mix of true stories and fabricated tales based on fact that you'll read, reread, and share her stories many times."

~ Amy Lyle, author, *The Amy Binegar-Kimmes-Lyle Book of Failures,* number one bestselling Amazon author in Humor & Entertainment; *We're All A Mess, It's OK;* filmmaker; and television host of *In the Burbs.*

The first part of this book, THE TATTLETALES, is a work of non-fiction.
Names, characters, places, and incidents are the recollections of the author, recounted in vignettes, and shared by permission
of the participants. Certain details may be altered in the
instances of those who wish to remain anonymous.

The second half of the book, THE SHENANIGANS, is purely fictional...sorta.

Teacher Tattletales

Dedication

Since this book is one by teachers, about teachers, and for
teachers, I'd like to recognize every principal that offered me a
teaching job. Without you, this book wouldn't be possible!
*In one's high school senior picture, there is sometimes a remark under the
photograph. Here are the comments that stand out in my mind about each:*

Dr. James R. Hallford, Redan High School principal
Superintendent of DeKalb County Public School System, Georgia
Walked softly; carried a big stick. He whistled while he
worked.

Mr. Robert Cresswell, Salem High School principal
Conyers, Georgia
"I don't chit-chat."

Mr. Terry Graff, Conyers Middle School, principal
Conyers, Georgia
He had the heartiest belly laugh.

Dr. Therese Reddekopp, Northgate High School,
principal

Newnan, Georgia
"We only hire the best at Northgate."

Special Recognition:
Mrs. Patricia DeVane, Memorial Middle School,
principal
Conyers, Georgia
"Here's to your best year yet!"

Thanks for taking a chance with me.

Table of Contents

Non-Fictional Tattletales

Southern Fictional Shenanigans

Elementary School

Big Mack

I attended elementary, middle, and high school with Mack Neal. He lived in town next door to one of my favorite girlfriends. There were lots of kids on their street. This girlfriend and I were attached at the hip. She was either at my house or I was at hers as we swapped off sleepovers on Friday nights all the way from elementary throughout high school. I liked her house better because her street had more kids to hang out with including her two-years-older sister and all her own friends. And the boys were cuter, too. We all met under the streetlights until we were called in and in the summer, that was always way after dark.

This decade, the 1960s, was a more innocent time and we all could be trusted, except for Dwayne, who was a hottie because he was really a year older but was held back a year in school so he was not only more physically built in 5th grade, he was knowledgeable, too, because he had much-older brothers and sisters. His reputation preceded him. But that's another story for another time.

One day in middle school, which we called junior high then, our teacher was absent and a male adult substituted for her. That was unusual. We mostly had female substitutes. We were respectful. There was not any misbehavior like trying to trick the sub. He called the roll to see who was in attendance and when he rounded the alphabet at the M/N's he called out Mack's name.

"McNeal?"

Mack answered, "Present." (Present? Really? That was some archaic terminology. We used to say stuff like that back then.)

The man said, "And what is your first name?"

Mack answered, "Mack."

The substitute responded, "What did you say? What is your first name?"

"My name is Mack Neal."

"No, son, I have your last name. What is your first name?" the man asked.

And so it went a while longer until the old man – a retired teacher himself - got it straight.

Mack Neal and I attended school together for twelve years, played as children under that lamppost in middle school, were in the same high school classes and clubs, and were forever entwined in our small town. When he signed my favorite and precious school yearbook for the last time, I thought he would be writing something so profound about all our years together. I thought he would bring up memories that I might have forgotten about in all our adventures. I thought he respected me so much that he would write a challenge for me to make something of myself in the years to come or how he expected me to excel in this or that in my future. That's what I remember writing in his yearbook for the final time – words of wisdom, advice, some achievement in our youth that would prove that we would go far in life and make each other and our community proud.

I looked forward to seeing those sentimental and heartfelt words written only for each other in our last year of high school. It was going to be special just like we wrote to every other person in our graduating class like, "Good Luck!", "Can't wait to get out of this place!" , "Our math teacher can go to H***!"

See? Kids of our era were famous for our unique verbiage.

And Mack's message to me was memorable. While reading it, I saw all the effort and thought he put into those last words that he'd probably never pen to me again which said, "It's been real. Mack."

Corn Dog Sticks

It started with Kindergarten Open House. My youngest and I were visiting his classroom and meeting his teacher before the first day of school.

And I was horrified.

She was supposed to be the best teacher in the kindergarten program. She had been a teacher in the building for several years but in another curriculum. This was her first year teaching five-year-old students and I could tell already we were not going to have a good year together. I taught pre-school for my church's kindergarten program for several years. We used these supplies: pencils, crayons, colored pencils, washable markers, regular markers, glue sticks, tape, pencil sharpener, pens, play dough, food coloring, sequins, glitter, stamp pads, sticky Velcro, dry erase markers, etc. which could all be used in science-art-writing-math-based lessons. Am I right? Of course I am.

So what does one wear to conduct all these tactile lessons? Certainly *not* hose, high heels, and a fancy dress. I don't care if it IS an open house. Dress as the teacher you want to personify…someone who came to *teach*. This was not the evening for the parents meet and greet. This was the *children's* Open House.

I wanted someone who was going to cuddle my snot-nosed child and make him feel good about himself; someone nurturing who might sit on the floor and get dirty with these five-year olds; someone who knew how to channel boys' frolicsome behaviors; someone who understood squirrelly boys who couldn't sit still. And this teacher just wasn't making the grade. I knew just by her appearance, she wasn't going to be hands-on.

I am an only daughter, so I can say this: having a female child is way different than boys. I am not saying it's any easier, just different. And her only child was a daughter.

I received notes home about our son's antics almost every day: "Your child stepped on another boy's shoelaces in the hall." "Your child did not come back from the playground after recess fast enough." But the real clincher was, "Your child put his corndog sticks up his nose at lunch." Really?

As a former high school teacher, what if I wrote a note home about some of my students' behaviors?

"Your tenth-grader blew his nose too loudly five times during the exam that we took which might have disturbed the other students and caused concentration problems."

"Your child was flirting with another girl in class when everyone in the school clearly knows that he is going steady with Pat Ann, the most popular girl in eleventh grade and who is a possible future Homecoming Queen, and this would absolutely break her heart if she knew."

"Your eighth-grader came to school this morning with a suck bump, or hickey, as some might call it, on his neck. We just thought you should know."

My own mother, a former teacher for thirty-seven years, commented, "Who has time to write that many notes every day and who is watching those other students when she does?"

Now, I didn't want to rock the boat any more than it already was by complaining all year to an administrator, but I was so pissed at this teacher's bias against boys that at the end of the school year I bought the book *BRINGING UP BOYS* by James Dobson, made an appointment with the principal of the school, handed my gift to him, and asked him to place it in the professional library at his school. And by the way, would he please recommend that his teachers read it before next school year? It was too late for us.

And then, as a Mama Bear, I finally wrote back:

"Dear Teacher,

You pointed out our son's behavior at lunch. I would like to put things in perspective. At least they were *his* corndog sticks and *his* nose."

There were worse things in life.

Going AWOL

My children have benefitted from the variety of schools there are for students. My youngest, *The Spare*, had attended more than my oldest. He started in Montessori, then went to public school, and finished in a private school situation. His older brother, *The Heir*, went all the way through public school, although at one time we considered a military private school plan. Not really, but we wanted him to think so during one low period. (To keep from embarrassing my children more than I already do, I dubbed them the same monikers that the British press gave Prince William and Prince Harry because of their birth order.)

With a first child, we didn't know what we were doing. I wasn't a good disciplinarian because I wasn't disciplined all that much while growing up. The only reason I tried to behave was not to disappoint my mother. The look on her face when she was disheartened with me was enough for me to toe the line. I've jokingly said she could have been a travel agent for guilt trips. I was strong-willed and was tough to handle, *in my opinion,* although I think she might have agreed, unless I wanted to please so as to not feel guilty about our differences.

For the most part, *The Heir* was an easy child to raise, however, we did have our moments and it was then I tried to slough off my parental responsibilities on to someone or something else. I didn't want to be the bad guy. Let someone else or a situation break the bad news of how he was supposed to behave.

However, when *The Spare* was a toddler, I became more creative in the discarding of my obligations. I told him his behavior was being observed by either the White Police (color of cars of the city's law enforcement), the Brown Police (color of cars of the county's law enforcement, or the Red Police (color of cars of emergency vehicles other than first responder vehicles or fire trucks). Very rarely there would be some regular red truck with a siren and light on its roof but when there was, I pointed it out, too.

If we went out to lunch or dinner and there was a uniformed officer having a meal at a nearby table, I would tell him to pay special attention to his behavior in this establishment because he was being watched by law enforcement. If there wasn't a uniformed officer, I just told him the other patrons had the authority to tattle on him and there was nothing I could do. I *never* said what would happen if they spoke to him. I left that up to his imagination. Wasn't that awful?

And how I treated our oldest son was about the same mindset. Around the end of the elementary school years and before middle school, there was a contest of wills between him and my husband and me. I did not want to deal with it, naturally. *Hubby* was out of town traveling that week for his job and it seemed I was up to bat as the enforcer, and that wasn't going to happen.

I wrote to several military boarding schools in Georgia and Alabama and over the course of the next week or so, we started receiving lots of pamphlets describing their school and how their programs could whip rascally boys into fine young men. Their brochures had beautiful pictures and came with testimonials, mottos, school objectives, and a history of their learning and discipline instruction at their institution. They all sounded great and were definitely pricey.

We were not going to send him away but I didn't tell him that. I just wanted to scare him a little so that he would comply with our household rules. I took all the brochures and scattered them neatly across the kitchen table as though I had been perusing them intently. My objective was for him to see them…and be nervous.

When he walked in the kitchen, he saw them, glanced over the material, turned to me and asked, "You can wear uniforms at these schools?" That question made sense as he never missed an opportunity in his formative years to don his Superman, Batman, Popeye, Dick Tracy, and Robin Hood garb.

I answered, "Yes."

"And you get to carry a gun?"

"I think so," I commented weakly as I was now feeling nervous with where this line of questioning was headed.

"Then, *sign me up!*"

Well, that sure backfired.

Different As Night and Day

President Carter's mother was known to all as Miss Lillian. In the south if a young person knows an older person well and needs to be respectful, their first names are preceded with 'Miss', 'Mrs.', 'Ms', or 'Mr.' Otherwise, if they do not know them all that well, they address them using their surnames. I grew up calling my mother's friends, Miss Martha Anne or Miss Doris.

Miss Lillian had nicknames for her two boys, too. One she called her PRIDE and the other she called her JOY. Do you think you can guess which son was assigned which name? These brothers materialized from the same parents but were as different as night and day. I, too, have two sons who are as dissimilar just as Jimmy and Billy Carter were.

Both my boys had the same wonderful pre-school teacher and teacher's assistant those special years. Because a classroom assignment was so precious, each year they continued instructing the identical student-designed Mother's Day present - a crayon drawing of their pupils' mothers with questions about her answered by the children and recorded by their teachers. It's funny to see their different descriptions of the moms. I framed mine and they hang in my bedroom. These are the answers of our boys who had the same set of parents and the same household. Look at how differently they saw me.

Here were the questions with their answers:

My mother has _____ hair and _____ eyes.
Oldest: My mother has blonde hair and green eyes.

Youngest: My mother has blonde hair and green eyes.

She is about ___feet tall.
Oldest: She is about 70 feet tall.
Youngest: She is about 6 feet tall.

Her favorite thing to do is_____.
Oldest: Her favorite thing to do is cook.
Youngest: Her favorite thing to do is to get her nails done.

She cooks very good _____ for me.
Oldest: She cooks very good tomato soup for me.
Youngest: She cooks very good meatball sandwich for me.

My mom is so nice and will _____ with me.
Oldest: My mom is so nice and will play toys with me.
Youngest: My mom is so nice and will bring back something for me.

The thing I like to do most with my mom is_____.
Oldest: The thing I like to do most with my mom is hug her.
Youngest: The thing I like to do most with my mom is fish together.

And like Miss Lillian, these boys are my PRIDE and JOY.

If you are a mother, have one, or know one, HAPPY MOTHER'S DAY!

My Friend, Flicka

When I was growing up, I loved horses. In elementary school, during the 1960s, I owned individual and sets of the Breyer Horse Collections. If you played with them, too, you might remember these miniature horses were glossy plastic. The company manufactured Arabian, Palomino, Appaloosa, Quarter horse, and Clydesdale miniature varieties. I named every one of my twenty-plus pint-sized horses and wrote their names with a magic marker on duct tape strips. I placed these strips on their bellies. Two names I still remember were King (a stallion) and Flame (a foal).

As an only child with an overactive imagination, I would entertain myself on long road trips. I pretended an imaginary horse was running along beside our car driven by one of my parents. The horse was harnessed, leashed, and tethered as I sat in the back seat and cracked my window down a bit so I could hold my hand out and hold on to my horse.

And my horse, (you would think I'd remember his name but I don't), was keeping up with us, too…on every long trip…at sixty miles per hour…at more than three hours a stretch…down expressways…over bridges…without food or water. Poor pony. Gives new meaning to the word, 'horsepower'.

My cousin had a horse once. I watched it bite her on the cheek when she and I were both about eight. Maybe that's one reason my parents never bought a pony for me. And besides, I could ride it whenever she did without the expense of owning one.

So, I had to fantasize. And my dreams lasted for a while. In third grade, a group of girls (never boys) played 'horse' at recess. We feigned to ride horses over jumps in an enclosed area. We collected broken branches and gathered rocks from the playground to build low-jumping fences all over the designated space in the schoolyard.

Recess must have been at least an hour, it seemed, because *every* day it took almost that long to 'rebuild' our horse hurdles. By the time we finished building and were ready to jump, we would have about five minutes left of our outdoor time and then we'd be called to come back for class.

I say 'rebuild' because the next day we would come out to play during our specific time and find that the fourth grade classes had destroyed all of our hard work when it was their turn to play outside after us in the same area. Bummed out, of course, we nevertheless reconfigured, jumped a bit, and then were called into the building when recess was over. I guess those fourth graders didn't like playing 'horse". It was like the movie *Groundhog Day*. We went outside, we built, we jumped, we left, and our space was torn down. Built, jumped, left, torn down. Why did we continue to put up with that?

But what else were we going to do? All we had on our 1960s playground were six swings and one slide. We had mastered those and we *were not* going to play with the boys. They had imaginary guns.

Chatty Cathy

My first grade teacher was older than dirt. She may not have been, but her fashion sense seemed to suggest it: old-fashioned hairstyle, plain eyeglasses (one style fits all), and her shoes that looked suspiciously orthopedic. But that's the 1950s for you. It doesn't help to look back at our first grade 1959 black and white class picture. So, of course her dress looked drab and gray. It might have been a colorful royal blue but I never paid attention then and now it was defined in the hues of the decade – light gray and dark gray. Her shoes could have been a rich camel brown, but they were clunky and thick, therefore were considered not stylish. Her eyeglasses looked like those that every other teacher that year who wore spectacles were sporting.

I was constantly moved from desk to desk because I was continually getting reprimanded for talking too much. I warmed every seat at every desk in my first-grade classroom. I never felt ashamed, really. I remember still loving elementary school and enjoyed getting up and getting dressed to go. Our first grade composite is a sight to behold. We've all changed in our extra sixty years since, yet I still recognize most.

I was a wiggly child who begat a wiggly child. I vented my frustration to a young former teacher friend of mine, and one who I knew would understand my problem and offer fresh insight like she always did to the youth in her church or in her high school where she taught. Because of her empathy and creative instruction, she was Teacher of the Year several times.

My reserved mother accused me of telling everything I knew to everybody. I couldn't help those thoughts that passed through my brain that I wanted to share. Ok, I am outspoken. I should edit my thoughts before I speak. I think, "I speak my mind because it hurts to bite my tongue". Then I say, "You know who else talks a lot and share her stories that always seem to make people feel better? Well, that's who I want to be like."

And my former educator and wonderful woman had just that knack. As I approached her about what to do about my squirrely son who was having trouble in kindergarten, she responded with an anecdote of her own to make me feel better about my child's situation. She told me her story about when she was a little girl about my son's same age. She was a real chatterbox herself and got in trouble because of it often. Her elementary school teacher and the principal of the school frowned upon this affinity of hers.

Her family lived in a rural area at the north end of the county and she attended its only primary school. This school was probably twelve miles from her home so she rode the bus early to make it to school on time. One day, like any other day, she chatted away and her teacher had enough, was exasperated, and didn't know how to keep her quiet for very long, so eventually sent her to the principal's office.

The principal thought maybe she should go home for the remainder of the day. He wanted to call her home and have her mother come pick her up but he was in a predicament. He knew her parents did not own a phone. So he called the family's neighbor's house. This neighbor walked across her yard to this child's home to inform the girl's mother that the principal telephoned and suggested that she come pick her daughter up from school. Now there was another dilemma. This girl's mother did not have a car. How was she supposed to retrieve her daughter?

This sweet neighbor loaned her automobile to her friend so she could drive to the school and pick up her child. During the ride home, my mentor said she wondered what her mother might say to her and what kind of trouble she might be in. She waited a long time on those back roads to her home for her mother to say something. Eventually her mother commented, "Honey, all this talking is going to make you an interesting adult."

And, it has.

Art Linkletter's "Kids Say The Darnedest Things!"

I was born and raised on 1950s television. Art Linkletter was the go-to host for a long list of radio and television shows even before I was born. In those days he was our Tom Bergeron (*Dancing with the Stars*, *America's Funniest Home Videos*), or Chris Harrison (*The Bachelor*, *The Bachelorette*, *Who Wants To Be A Millionaire*?), or even Dunwoody, Georgia native, Ryan Seacrest who has hosted many television and radio shows (*American Idol*, *Live with Kelly and Ryan*, and more).

While hosting *House Party* both on radio and television, from January 1945 to September 1969, the show's best-remembered segment was "Kids Say the Darndest Things". Linkletter interviewed an estimated 23,000 schoolchildren between the ages of five and ten during the segment's almost-three-decade run.

Life was pretty tame back then and so were the television programs, so questions like "Where do babies come from?" would never have crossed host Art Linkletter's lips, I wouldn't think so anyway. Between five and nine I was naïve, too. I didn't have an older sister to pass down such knowledge. I lived in an only child bubble. But by the time I was in fourth grade and ten years old, my best friend, Gayle, who had a sister two years older than herself, inquired if I knew.

Sex Education wasn't offered until middle school. We had to learn about the birds and the bees from our family, whether that is your parents or older siblings. My mother hadn't had the talk with me yet, although my body was changing early and I ended up becoming a woman when I was twelve. I had to learn it all from Gayle, who heard the talk from her sister, a *sixth-grader*, and *who knows* where she heard it.

And so here we were and I am sure I looked like a deer in headlights when she posed the question. Later, I heard of some creative answers from mothers (or fathers) to this question. One mother recalled panicking when she heard her child asking for the answer to life's biggest mystery at a young age and blurted out, "The dryer."

Another parent commented, "One way to get around it is to use scientific words to this query. Since they will not know the meanings to these immense words, you can say you answered honestly without saying much because they will not know what you are talking about. My child became bored with this conversation and left the room before the end of the discussion."

One person wrote that her mother replied, "Down under" and so for five years this child thought babies came from feet. Absurd. But remember, the answer wasn't specific. Another remark from a mother said, "The clearance rack at Wal-Mart."

Are dads' answers any better? One wrote, "I asked my dad and he said there was a magical bean you could buy from Wal-Mart and my mom ate one and she puked me out nine months later." She believed that story until she took her puberty classes in middle school. And what's with Wal-Mart being a part of the explanations on procreation?

Another child posed the reproduction question to his dad and his father answered, "The cabbage patch." This youngster went to his garden daily to check on the cabbages to see if anything was taking place to produce a brother or sister. His mother became sad watching his faithful visits and finally told him, "Your dad's a liar."

I answered Gayle's question. I shared that I always thought babies were checked out from the hospital like library books. Whenever I visited the hospital with my mother, I saw that the babies - all lined up and laid out next to each other in rows in the nursery…looked *just like books*.

Since 1996, there has been help, though, to get through this quandary. All that's needed to be said was/is, "Go watch Animal Planet."

Behave Yourself

I tried; believe me when I say this, I really did. Growing up, I felt confined when I had to adhere to rules. I tried to behave, but sometimes it was just my nature to be a non-conformist. I don't think I had been diagnosed as having an "artist's temperament" yet. I was just trouble for my mother, I'm sure. Nothing totally alarming, I just wasn't very compliant. Her friends were surely saying she had lost control.

I also tried to get organized as an adult and set a good example as a parent. Life for my children was full during the elementary school years – baseball, basketball, and soccer practices, piano lessons, scouts, and church activities. I thought if I set up a behavioral/organizational chart, it would help not only *The Heir* but also *me*. We'd both be systematized. If there was a chart in this bathroom, in the form of a calendar with expectations, homework/project assignment due dates, and extra-curricular activities dates and times, he would be able to see what his short-term future (like a week's worth) was. He would then be able to know what to expect and plan to get all these things done that week…and get to bed at a decent time after he checked off his day's or week's expectations. Then he'd be compensated and would be proud of himself. We would include rewards like stickers, stars, treats, and privileges. I could be proud of me, too, as I was determined to get our lives in order.

This attempt lasted two weeks.

That first week, I tried to follow-through with doing things on a set schedule. I focused on all those rewards for the accomplishments during those seven days. Maybe my parents rewarded me as a child for my performances but there certainly wasn't a chart in the 1950s and 1960s. As a free spirit, I was made to feel shame when I did not.

When it came time for *The Spare* to be under rule with charts and graphs, I just didn't even attempt it. His fourth grade teacher encouraged me in a parent conference one time to set one up and I just looked at her and said, "I can't." She looked puzzled. "What do you mean, you can't?" she asked. I then explained about the first child's scenario and how it didn't work, not so much for him but for me, and that I wondered what kind of example I was setting if my children saw that I couldn't follow through on goals. I thought that kind of behavior would be worse. Do as I say, not as I do? What kind of lesson was that?

And so guess what I didn't do?

Lies Our Mothers Told Us...and Dads, too

Recently, a friend wrote this on her Facebook page: "My mother once taught me that if I ate sweets before noon, I'd get worms. Uh-oh."

This set off a firestorm of texts regarding what lies our parents once told us before middle school and we could figure these things out ourselves. We may have even said a few to our youngsters. I've divided them up into categories. Are you guilty of any of these? I know that if not these, there are others I've been known to fabricate.

Things That Have to Do with Your Body:
"If you swallow watermelon seeds, you will grow a watermelon in your tummy."

"You need to rest 30 minutes after eating before swimming or you'll drown."

"If you eat fat off a steak, it will make your hair shine."

"If you drink your milk, you'll grow big and tall!"

"Shaving your legs makes the hair grow back thicker."

Don't Touch That!:
"Touching frogs will give you warts."

"When we went to the store my mom used to tell me, 'Every time you touch something a kitten dies.'"

Holidays and Festivities:
"Santa is watching you."

"As a kid I put a tooth in a plastic bag and slid it under my pillow for the tooth fairy. When my parents forgot to put money under my pillow, my dad said,

'You shouldn't have put the tooth in a bag. The tooth fairy couldn't smell it.'"

"Living on the West Coast, my friend showed the East Coast feed of the New Year's Eve countdown to her kids and she had them in bed a little after nine."

Things You Shouldn't Do:

Me: "I want to because Gayle (my friend) is going to." Mother: "If Gayle jumped off a bridge, would you?"

"If you cross your eyes, they will stay that way." Or "If you keep making that face, it'll freeze that way."

"If you have a wart it's because you peed in the street."

"Cracking your knuckles will give you arthritis."

"Watching TV too close to the screen will make you go blind."

"Dropping a penny from the Empire State Building can kill someone."

"If you swallow gum, it takes seven years to digest."

Pets:

"My uncle told my cousin her turtle could do tricks like play dead. They went through 7 turtles."

"When my dog died, my parents told me that she was at the doggie nursing home and visitors weren't allowed."

"My father always said the animals on the side of the road were just taking a nap because the road was warm."

"My dad told me my dog left to be with my father's mother in Japan, when he actually died. I mean, what?"

Let's Calm Down:

"We're almost there!" amidst a painfully long road trip.

The classic "I'll check on you in a minute" as you say good night.

"We'll come back another time."

"It won't hurt. I promise!"

"We'll see."

Flat Out Lies:

"When the ice cream truck plays the music, that means it's out of ice cream."

"I never would have done that when I was your age."

"My roommate grew up on a farm and was told by her parents that their TV only worked when it rained."

"My mom told me 7-Eleven was only open from 7 p.m. to 11 p.m., and that 7 p.m. was far too late to have a Slurpee."

"When I was a kid my parents warned me that if I pressed the 'reset' button on the power outlet the house would explode."

And of course, the one we have all said, "I'm leaving without you!"

Name Calling

Did you have a hard time naming your children?

When I hear from teachers, they especially find it hard to name one of their own after teaching a few rascals so that they wouldn't *dare* use the names of those students for their own. They might turn out like those little hooligans!

I enjoyed the book *Freakanomics* by Steven D. Levitt and Stephen J. Dubner. The subtitle is *A Rogue Economist Explores the Hidden Side of Everything*. It redefines the way we look at the modern world.

Chapter Six's title is "Perfect Parenting, Part II; or: Would a Rhoshanda by Any Other Name Smell as Sweet?" The topic is that "the belief in parental power is manifest in the first official act a parent commits: giving the baby a name. As any modern parent knows, the baby-naming industry is booming, as evidenced by a proliferation of books, websites, and baby- name consultants. Many parents seem to believe that a child cannot prosper unless it is hitched to the right name; names are seen to carry great aesthetic or even predictive powers."

Is naming destiny?

With our firstborn, we had a heck of a time. I found the book *Parents Book of Baby Names* by Martin Kelly. It contained the origins and history, their meaning, the nick- names, and derivations of hundreds of female and male names. But then *Freakanomics* made me think—can a name be damaging to one's psyche?

I asked my friends on Facebook to tell me about actual people they know/knew that I could add to the list. These are real people, folks. Remember that while reading. Here they are:

Crystal Fountain was a schoolmate.

Miss White married Mr. Green and moved to Gray, Georgia.

Another White gal, Bonnie, married Ken Knight. Did you figure out she was then Bonnie White Knight?

Dr. Strait was a Cartersville, Georgia orthodontist.

Jimmy Shivers' father was in the refrigeration business.

A friend's parents' actual names are Dick and Jane.

Someone knows a Jay Bird.

Sonny, Dusty, Wendy, Stormy, and Misty Williams.

A friend worked with a girl named Holly Bush.

Jazzercise instructor had an aunt named Kat Knapp and her daughter-in-law was Nita Knapp.

A neighbor knew a girl in high school named Polly Sachs—pronounced Socks. Her middle name was Esther. Now say it all together…that's right, polyester socks!

I went to college with a Twinkle Starr. Twinkle was born April 1.

A preschool teacher said she went to school with a guy named Rusty Carr.

A high school teacher graduated with a Honey Buns.

One of my flight attendant friends knows a Lulu.

There is a Bob from Tyty, Georgia.

An octogenarian in the neighborhood went to school with Ima June Bugg.

A former choir member of mine knew a Safety Furst and he was a doctor in Oklahoma.

A high school girlfriend knew a Brick Stone.

And here's a grand finale name:
A good friend mentioned to me about his friend, Bubba. You know, Bubba is a great Southern name. It usually comes from someone younger in a family calling a male sibling, like a brother, Bubba because they can't say brother. And so it sticks. If you live in the South, you probably know *lots* of Bubbas. But these big brothers grow up. Johnny turns into John. Ricky turns into Rick. Billy turns into Bill. But what do Bubbas do? This Bubba turned into a Delta airline captain. He realized how unprofessional it would be if he kept his common name as they announced over the intercom to the passengers, "Ladies and gentlemen, today you will be in the good hands of Captain Bubba."

The Age Old Debate of Nature vs. Nurture

Which weighs more heavily?

This philosophical issue is one of the oldest and even today different branches of psychology still take sides in the debate. Is nature (genetics/biological influences) more important or should nurture (the impact of the environment) be the primary focus of behavior?

All the genes and hereditary factors that influence who we are is nature. It includes our physical appearance all the way through our personality quirks, while nurture refers to the environmental variables, which include our early experiences in childhood, how we were raised, our social relationships, and our surrounding culture that impact who we are.

Both of my boys attended our private church pre-kindergarten program. Because of the excellent reports about the curriculum, it was a tough nut to crack to gain admittance. The waiting list each year was long for each of the two-year, three-year, and four-year-old programs. Church members were bumped to the front of the lineup.

But I still wondered if I answered the application incorrectly would my firstborn still have a chance of getting in because one of the questions was "What kind of discipline do you use for your child to monitor behavior?" Uh, oh. Since I am unorthodox about many things, I worried I might have hurt his chances because I answered on the line provided, "Whatever works."

I loved this pre-school program so much that after my oldest graduated and moved on to public school kindergarten, I took a job teaching one of the three-year-old programs. The wait-list was so long because of the good reputation, they opened up a second class and I applied.

I hadn't planned on 'testing' the three-year-olds in my class about nature verses nurture; it just happened. In the back of my playroom was a section for make-believe. Part art area, part music area, and part house area. In the house area was a fantasy kitchen. There was a child-sized refrigerator, ironing board, wood iron, table, plastic food, mops, brooms, chairs, baby dolls, cribs, etc. There was nothing masculine about this location – all feminine touches. I'd like to think that the boys received their turn with the outdoor sandboxes, trucks, pails, shovels, and such. The two areas were not meant to segregate the children. As a matter of fact, both offered many activities to every child.

But this is what I found interesting. While the boys played in the child-sized kitchen, even with all the female gender type elements, these little boys took the mops and brooms and pretended they were machine guns and rifles. Three-year-old male babies!

So, I conducted an experiment. I knew these families. I knew these boys were firstborns. I knew (but asked anyway) if their parents allowed them to watch only age appropriate television shows without aggression (Affirmative). And yet, their behaviors were innately masculine.

It was just simple sample – maybe six male students. But it told me a lot. Even though today, most experts recognize that both factors play a critical role and that nature and nurture interact in important ways all throughout life. But I had the St. John scientific theory method to tell me what's what at the age of three. That experiment was genetically engineered. Life would nurture them later on.

My own personal experience included reading to both my boys and I thought that Richard Scarry's books were the best. My oldest loved all the pages. My youngest gravitated to just his favorites. Whereas I wanted to read *Great Big Schoolhouse*, he wanted me to read *Cars and Trucks from A-Z.* I was not all that interested in them but we both got what we wanted...I'd read a page from my favorite (about school) and he'd get his turn (about vehicles.) One day I asked him why he liked that book so much. He answered, "I like the way they sound." He was two going on three. He hadn't much experience in hearing motors like that, but his dad did as he grew up liking motorized vehicles. But there you go. Nature?

What would you call it?

A Day in the Life of a Teacher

Elementary School Version

Arriving to school in the 1990s, teachers must go to the mailroom to sign in and record their attendance. There was a pencil, tied to a string, on a clipboard with the attendance sheet.

So as a friend of mine who taught health and physical education was performing this morning ritual, there sat one of her favorite kindergarten students. This lovely was a sweet girl although not the sharpest crayon in the box. Assuming she was sick because she was already up at the front office so early, the teacher inquired as to why she was there. This student proudly piped up and enthusiastically said, "I'm going home! I've got *lice*."

This Health and P.E. teacher thought, "Is this how my day is going to go?" She had no idea what lay in store however.

She approached her office in the gym where she taught her classes. Half the year she taught physical education and the other half was health class. This time of year was for physical exercise…volleyball, dodgeball, basketball, and the like. Students started filing in before the tardy bell rung. A few brought notes of excuses up to her as she marked students present in her attendance book. She started reading notes and chuckled to herself because of the creative rationalizations of parents trying to have their child dismissed from any physical exertion in class that day. A few read:

"Please excuse Tiffany from PE today. She has a swole face."

"My child can't dress out today because it is her time of the munt."

"Larry can't dress out today. It rained last night."

Her day didn't get much better.

Later that morning, her co-worker began choking and coughing in the presence of a female custodian. This teacher was rather out of breath from all the coughing. This custodian, who was working along beside them sweeping the perimeters of the gym floor while class was in session, said, "Am I going to have to do the Heineken Remover on you?" Her female co-worker started another having another fit – this time laughing which turned into coughing again.

While this was happening, an assistant principal approached this same custodian and asked her if he could see the bottom of her tennis shoes. A student was missing her expensive shoes from the locker room the day before and reported it to the office. To be able to identify her own shoes should this happen, she had written her name on the bottom. The assistant principal asked the cleaning woman to please lift up her feet and show her the soles of the shoes that looked like the ones missing, and sure enough, they had the real owner's name on them. Of course the custodian was escorted to the office to get to *bottom* of it (pun intended) but was heard saying it was "an accident" or some such nonsense.

Maybe they needed some witnesses for the "theft" or the "mistake" because there was shortly an intercom announcement to the entire school, "Will all teachers with aides report to the theater?"

With one of the health teachers out absent and the front office not able to find a substitute teacher for the day, teachers sometimes had to cover for other teachers during their own planning period. So my friend had to cover for a co-worker towards the end of her day. Knowing the curriculum for fifth-grade health, she was able to pick up where the students had left off the day before: Introducing Good Eating Habits. She was telling these students about the different types of meats by using euphuisms – poultry/chicken, beef/cow, veal/calf, bison/buffalo, etc. Some of the students had never heard of these synonyms but seemed eager to learn. She mentioned that one boy in the class raised his hand to inform that he'd had bison for dinner the night before. When she asked him how he liked it, he asked her, "Haven't you ever had buffalo wings?"

Her own fifth grade son came into her room after school and was so proud of himself. Being the son and grandson of teachers, he had a strong vocabulary because this teacher and her mother didn't dummy down their own vocabulary in their conversations with him. When a fellow student in his class didn't understand a word while the teacher was describing something and would ask her to define it, she'd then turn to my friend's own son and ask him to give the definition because he always knew all the vocabulary questions that were asked of him. Instead of a dictionary, he was the "go-to" resource and he had been called on again that day.

She elaborated that just because the school bell dismissed the children at the end of the day, that didn't mean the stories stopped; she was still confronted with more. Her own children attended the same school where she taught. That afternoon her youngest son, who was in the first grade, asked her, "Who is Anita?" She had no idea who he was referring to and asked him for more information. He said, "Before we left school today, they asked over the intercom for Anita's mop and bucket." She said she thought about this and it finally dawned on her that what the office was really announcing that afternoon was, "I need a mop and bucket in room twenty-three."

Later that evening before bedtime, her third-grade son announced that he thought that a boy in his class, Joseph, "thinks he's so special!" She asked him, "Why?" He answered, "He was absent from school a few days and today when he came back, he was bragging about having his dad in a vase on their mantle." Of all the funnies that happen on any given school day, this is the sad side: a young third-grade student had lost his father in a car wreck.

Explaining what that really meant, Joseph and his family were in their prayers before the lights went out.

Middle School

Calling Roll

No matter how hard teachers wish for the first few days of school to operate smoothly, there were always blips. There were so many names to learn when you are teaching older students because of all the class changes. While teaching gifted middle school students, the state department of education mandated they be served 4 ½ hours a week.

There were several ways to accommodate the students. They could be pulled out of their regular classrooms for about 45 minutes every day for the week or pulled out for longer periods of time for fewer days, or they could be pulled out for one day a week for the entire required time. We chose the latter. That meant the first day of class happened in week one. The second day of class met during week two, and so it went with the third week, fourth, and so on.

Since I taught gifted students in elementary, middle, and high school, I participated in all three types of delivery. Elementary school was two or three days a week and high school was every day of block scheduling for a semester. Even then, in one of the high schools I taught, it took me a while to realize that I thought I saw this one student more often than the others. I soon realized he was a twin and I had both boys on roll but in different classes.

My middle school faculty loved the one day a week pull-out. The regular education kids would "rise to the top" the days the superior intellectual kids were gone and remedial kids could get double lessons on certain subjects.

While in middle school, my classroom had desks with chairs that slid underneath the tabletop. I also had an extra long sofa for some rest and relaxation (maybe separation at times, too). Several over achievers rushed to class on time to playfully struggle over who was going to sit on the sofa that day. With our smaller classes, everyone seemed to get a turn.

But remember, I was not seeing those kids daily either. And those first few class times were difficult to remember names as you wouldn't see them again for a week and in the meantime, a slew of other middle school grade level kids were in class.

As I took roll the first week in middle school, I recorded my attendance in my spiral attendance book and then taught little lessons where an easy oral quiz would give me their first grades in my gradebook. It also let them know we were getting down to business by staying focused right from the first day when they arrived to class. As each pupil answered some of my questions, I added a grade in my handwritten, not electronic, 1994 gradebook. The assignment was entitled "Oral Participation" with the date at the top of the column.

A week passed and I saw the same students again. While calling roll, I called out the name Robert. No answer. I called the rest of the roll and then went back to Robert's name. No answer again. I asked the class if they knew where Robert might be. They answered that there was not a Robert in our class. Now these students were in the seventh grade and had gone to school together for some time and were also in the same gifted classes the preceding year. They all knew each other and I thought they might be pulling my leg or that there really was not a student with that name.

I said, "There was a Robert last week." They all just looked at each other like I was nuts and, of course, nodded to each other that they were correct in answering there was no such person. No Robert last week. No Robert this week. And they were right – no Robert *at all*.

But I was so dumbfounded with myself. I thought for sure there was a student with that name the week before. Not only did I remember what he looked like, where he sat on the sofa, but I also had given him an "Oral Participation" grade. That rascal!

Robert must have been smart, too, because he made a 100 on that assignment.

To The One I Love

When I was in eighth grade, we were learning the parts of the formal letter and practicing writing letters, which we now know is a dying art form. Penmanship has gone by the wayside, too. I still like written notes and always encouraged everyone in my family to write a thank you note: it's mannerly, it's proper, and it's Southern.

While we were dissecting the parts of the letter in class – the greeting, the body, and the salutation – my teacher asked us to compose one for homework. I was sitting at my kitchen table while my mother was preparing dinner. She kept one eye on cooking and another eye on what I was doing for homework. She observed for a while and then said, "Let me tell you a story about a letter that your father sent to me."

I said, "OK."

She began, "We exchanged lots of letters during World War II. Your father was in the Navy on a destroyer on the outskirts of Italy. Because it was such a tempestuous time, he had to be careful of what he wrote in his letters. And so did I. It was scary because the war office would make sure the letters sent from the military did not carry any information in them that might be intercepted and used against the United States. There was a saying at that time and it was, 'Loose lips, sink ships.'"

She had my attention.

"One time," she continued, "I received a letter from your father that started just like your greeting part of the letter, 'Dear Darling', and after that, the entire body of the letter was totally cut out! But it had a salutation at the bottom and he signed it, 'Love,

Your Husband.' I thought to myself, 'What did he say? Were there valuable secrets about his mission in the letter? Will he get into trouble?'"

My eyes widened.

"Of course, I wrote back as quickly as I could, yet worried the entire time, weeks on end, about what was in his letter. Finally, I heard from him again. His answer about the previously cut-out center part of his letter? He said he knew he owed me a letter, he didn't have much time to write, wanted to let me know he was fine and safe, and he just cut out the middle part of the paper all by himself."

Mother kept that correspondence along with all her others from Daddy. Later when they both passed, I saw those keepsakes and was touched by the lovely romantic ones Daddy had sent to her. And now I am the keeper of their memories.

Brain Dead

To become middle school certified, one needed to take a course called "The Middle School Learner." That course taught you about the mindset of eleven to fourteen-year-olds. One of the major concepts I remembered learning was the term and definition of "brain dead." You've heard it. You've probably said it. But did you know it came from a real educational idea?

It did not mean "brain-dead" as in "A brain-dead individual has no clinical evidence of brain function." This "brain-dead" idea came from the journals of doctors in the field of education. We learned prior to the middle school years, a child's brain worked at around 80% capacity and the body worked at about 20%. The middle school age brain flipped-flopped…20% brain and 80% body which was trying to catch up.

Our middle school gifted students took yearly field trips to educational and yet fun locations. We went to Old Salem and the Reynolda House Museum of American Art in Winston-Salem, North Carolina. The museum displays American art ranging from the colonial period to the present. The home, built in 1917, was once owned by R.J. Reynolds, founder of the R.J. Reynolds Tobacco Company and his wife, Katharine Smith Reynolds and the dwelling was surrounded by formal gardens, shops, and restaurants.

One year we traveled to Huntsville, Alabama to the U.S. Space and Rocket Center. The space camp program incorporated real-world application of science, technology, engineering, and math. Our students prepared to become lunar explorers, spacecraft designers/mission controllers, and astronauts as they explored simulated moon walks in a 1/6th gravity chair and experienced what it was like to work in a frictionless environment manned by the maneuvering unit. They built and launched a two-stage model rocket and gained teamwork and management skills.

Another year we took a trip to Charleston, South Carolina where we slept on the aircraft carrier, The Yorktown, visited graveyard haunts at night, rode horse-drawn buggy tours over the historic cobblestone streets during the day, and had a scavenger hunt to find historical places and relics.

Every trip was a 3-day event.

One of the mothers of our students told the story about how her family went back to Charleston for a vacation about three years after her daughter's school trip. The girl, who was fourteen years old on our class trip, was now seventeen for her family excursion. Her mother commented to me how her daughter was "*ooooohhhing*" and "*aaaahhhhing*" all over the place in Charleston. She said her daughter commented about how she "loved this street" or "loved this house" or "loved this graveyard", or *whatever*. She expressed excitement about everything Charleston had to offer.

Her mother said to her, "Sweetie, you act like this is the first time you've ever seen this place. You came here on your gifted class trip just three years ago."

Her seventeen-year-old looked at her and said, "Oh. This is where we were?"

And this young lady graduated from Tufts in Boston!

Bless her heart. She was the victim of the adolescent "brain-dead" theory.

The World's Largest Outdoor Cocktail Party

I was on national television. Yep. And not just some blip on the screen. From what I was told, it lasted about thirty seconds. There was at least enough time for people I knew all across the United States to recognize me and later call me to tell me they had seen me. When I heard about being seen on TV, I was scared to get that recognition. I feared I was going to be in trouble. You see, I was a new teacher that year of momentary national notoriety and I was nervous about it because I had *skipped school*.

I called in sick.

In my defense, I really was sick! First year teachers caught many of their students' illnesses. I had the flu and I was sick as a *dawg* – I mean, dog – but I wasn't about to miss the 1978 Georgia-Florida football game in Jacksonville, Florida. I only had been teaching three months when I called that early Friday morning to inform the front office staff that I had the flu and couldn't come in. In the 1970s, we were not responsible for finding a sub at the last minute. The office was a treasure-trove of substitute teacher contacts.

As sick as I was, my date wasn't going to let me out of my commitment with him. The tickets were hard to come by, the seats were great, and even if I was sick, he told me I was going. We took a Winnebago with three other couples and he reassured me I could stay in the back away from everyone and rest. Yeah, right. We were both big Georgia fans and I didn't want to miss this opportunity to be a part of the big game even if I wasn't at my best. If the other couples weren't concerned about my being contagious, why should I?

We drove down Friday morning after my early phone call to my school and I did rest a little. I rallied some later that day and by Saturday, I soldiered into the game where our close-to-the-field and near-the-student-section seats were. Surely my rum and coke would help me get well – or at least feel better. I was told before I packed for the weekend to bring my own flask. No one watched or cared that you carried your flask full of alcohol into the stadium in 1978 – especially when attending the 'World's Largest Outdoor Cocktail Party'.

We had aisle seats and the next thing I remembered there was a cameraman in front of us on the steps in the aisle holding his mobile camera. We were no more than eight feet away from this guy. I saw him point the hand-held camera at us, but what I didn't know was there were little flashing green lights indicating that it was *live*!

My *Almost-Big-Sister's* husband was watching the game at their home. She was in her kitchen when she heard him yell, "Honey, get in here and see who is on TV!" She told me later that her reaction was, "Well, if I quit what I am doing and go in there now, by the time I make it, the person won't be on the screen anymore." So, she didn't go.

Ten seconds passed. Then she heard, "Really! Get in here! Look who's on TV!" Again, she didn't leave the kitchen where she was coordinating lunch because she thought that it was improbable that she'd make it into the den to see whoever it was on television.

More time passed. Finally, he screamed, "Hurry up! She's still on TV!" In the middle of a putting together a recipe, she left without wiping her hands and sure enough, she was right. She walked in and my time was up.

I did not mind being seen on TV except by *one* person: my principal. I really hoped he wasn't a Bulldog or Gator fan. Nothing was ever said when I returned to school on Monday morning.

How many times do I have to tell you? *I really was sick!*

Don't Stand So Close To Me

By sixth grade, we moved out of the only white elementary school in the county to the only white junior high school in the county. It stood in a separate building behind the high school campus where a breezeway connected the upper grades to the lower grades. Since my mother taught in the main building where the high school stood, I now rode to school with her, which meant I arrived at school early so she could welcome and monitor the behavior of her students when they entered her homeroom. After she parked her car in the teacher parking (a perk for me as it was closer to my junior high building) she would go her way and I'd go mine.

Before school started one day in my sixth grade homeroom, my teacher, who appeared to be at least seventy years old disappeared from the room for a moment. She had the same dress code as my first grade teacher. Styles must not have changed much in five years, at least for adults. And even if she looked old in appearance, she was the sweetest thing. She left a few of us girls giggling and drawing on her chalkboard. I don't know what the boys, who started drifting into the classroom, did that morning. Maybe they played paper football. You remember, paper football was also called finger football. It was a tabletop game loosely based on American football. The "football" was really a sheet of paper folded into a small triangle and it slid back and forth across a desk or a table by the flick of the finger between two opponents. If the triangular shaped paper-made 'football' passed a certain point without falling off the table, one 'scored'; then it was flicked over upright handmade-thumbs-up goal posts for the extra point.

Or maybe they were making cootie-catchers. If you don't know what those activities are, Google them.

In 1965, blackboards were made of slate and the erasers were made of felt. They might be called blackboards but some were green. Dry erase boards (or whiteboards), dry-erase pens or markers, and dry-erasers did not come into use until the 1990s. My girlfriends and I had a grand time just drawing pictures, erasing them, inhaling chalk dust (because the boards were so dusty), and drawing more pictures to entertain ourselves before the school bell rang to start the day.

I practiced drawing my letters in script on the chalkboard. I accentuated the curve of the letter with shadows, enhanced the script by adding doodles on the end of the letters…just about
anything to make my writing flourish and look pretty. I was standing and writing on the board beside a girl who I had known since first grade. She was a nice girl so I didn't understand her mean streak that morning. Everything I designed on the board, she erased it right in front of me. If I made a beautiful curly-q on some letter, she howled with laughter while she wiped-out my hard work. I drew another beautiful rendition of a letter and, again, my designs were eradicated. She snickered the entire time! Naturally, this began to annoy me.

"Please stop!" (Giggle, giggle was her comeback.)

"Stop it!" (Not a chance.)

My ire grew. I decided to answer her with the only thing a genteel little sixth grade girl knew to do:

I plowed my fist into her face! There I stood all girly-girl myself in a dress (no slacks in 1965). I looked sweet as sugar except for my knuckles, which turned red from the direct hit to her cheek. That stopped her alright. But then, while looking frozen for a moment, she started another kind of howling: this time with tears.

Our teacher came in and took eyewitness statements from the rest of our classmates who watched the boxing match in the room. I did not deny it. I personally didn't find anything really wrong with it. Luckily, there was not a behavior policy for that sort of thing with the school system. Or maybe there was. But I bet it didn't mention *girls* throwing the punches. Of course, my teacher told my mother but I was never punished by the teacher or principal. I don't even remember being punished by my mother. I just apologized and that was it.

And the best news of all, I still landed the first job I ever applied for. There was never anything in my permanent record about the incident even though they always told you everything you did wrong would be placed there for evidence.

Character Witness

While teaching our Mystery Unit for seventh graders, I used a lot of hands-on assignments to enhance the lesson. This unit was probably one of my favorite lesson plans. I grew up reading *Nancy Drew* and still love a good mystery. I re-established a connection with two of my high school friends who both worked for the city police department and the county sheriff's department. Both came to talk to my students about their experiences in law enforcement. They told of the crimes they had solved and some of the methods of catching the perpetrators.

When they visited in the 1990s, there was no such thing as the ID Channel (Investigative Discovery). I watched *Unsolved Mysteries* all the time. It aired from 1987 – 2002, first as specials and then as a regular series. Raymond Burr (who had been the lead in *Perry Mason* from 1957 – 1966) and Karl Malden (star of *Street of San Francisco* which ran from 1972-1977) were the hosts of the specials. Robert Stack (Elliott Ness, *The Untouchables* 1959 – 1963) hosted the regular series on NBC from 1988 – 1997, CBS from 1997-1999, and *Lifetime* from 2001 – 2002. I was a crime junkie. These law enforcement officers told tales about how they could get plump fingerprints off of a dried-up dead body or how prisoners were treated in our county jail, etc. We actually visited the newly built jail where offenders were housed. That visit was *too much information* for the students and *me*.

Usually I pretended to have "dead" bodies in the classroom with hidden clues scattered throughout the "crime scene". Prepared (and coached) volunteer witnesses were interviewed to establish a timeline determining what happened to the 'deceased' on the floor. The 'body' was usually an assistant principal who had to lie there for at least an hour while a bunch of twelve-year-olds stepped over and prodded the prone figure to get the administrator to laugh. This exercise usually coordinated with our middle school students reading, *And Then there Were None* by Agatha Christie. High school students didn't mind a little fun either like this with their required reading, *In Cole Blood* by Truman Capote.

Another exercise my *Co-Teacher* and I prepared was learning how to write a detailed eyewitness account from a demonstration. Its purpose was to help students to learn how important it was to learn to write in detail. Once we had approval from the administration, we coordinated with our police department, to have a plain-clothed policeman disrupt our class for a few seconds by running through the room, causing a mild disturbance while we were teaching a lesson, steal something from a student, and run out never to be seen again. Remember – this was the 1990s. Our town, our county, and our world was not a scary place at that time.

During this demonstration we wondered had the students paid close enough attention and noticed details about the event so that they could describe it well in an eyewitness identification report? One year, a sweet twelve-year old male student jumped out of his seat, ran to my desk, extended his arms in a defense mode, and tried to protect me from harm as the 'perpetrator' ran past me. Such chivalry! I still wet my pants even though I *knew* the day and time we had set up this 'criminal' activity.

On another day when our culprit was to visit, my *co-teacher* and I, without drawing attention to ourselves, cleared a path for the upcoming action. Sometime during that lesson, the individual ran into our class, darted around the room, stole a book off a student's desk, cradled it under his arm, and with a tremendous burst of speed, leaped over an empty desk and ran out of the other door in our two-room classroom.

A few moments later, while the students were still in shock, a uniformed officer walked into our classroom, introduced himself, and handed out the eyewitness identification report to our students. What could they remember and describe? The finished reports were hilarious. There were discrepancies from each student. This is the collection of details in describing the intruder: white, black, Hispanic, Chinese, anywhere from 5'2" to 6'4", thin, fat, bald, wearing a hat, glasses, red hair, you name it…when in reality he was African-American, 5'10", husky build, around thirty-five years old, thick black curly hair, wore jeans with a plaid shirt.

When he grabbed a student's book and left, the students also commented he stole: a winter cap, a book, several books, an atlas, a girl's jacket, and an eraser. But my favorite was "A football player carrying a football under his arm ran through the room."

No Stone Left Unturned

Since our gifted program was interdisciplinary and not serving the students just in one subject, we tried not to copy what was being taught in their regular education classrooms, but still stick to the county curriculum. Seventh graders were taught life sciences in their classrooms. Because I enjoyed adding humor to most situations, I wanted to really surprise my middle school learners. I designed a lesson for them to make it memorable, but not in a pretty way, but a rather PG-13 rating shocking way. I knew from previous years, students in this preteen age group loved to be grossed out. I took a good bit of information from a book titled *The Almanac of the Gross,Disgusting, & Totally Repulsive ~ a compendium of fulsome facts* by Eric Elfman. And, it was gross.

Man, this was stuff I didn't really want to know. I have never kept my toothbrush exposed on my bathroom counter since. It stated that the bathroom is the grossest room in the house and is constantly being assaulted by dangerous bacteria each time one flushed the toilet. Each flush consisted of a fine mist consisting of billions of water droplets which rise into the air. Hundreds of thousands of these contain bacteria from our intestines and land on every surface of the bathroom – you know, your doorknob, your floor, your cabinets, your sink, and especially your toothbrush. Did you really want to know that? Either you are welcome or I am sorry. Although they pretended not to like it, they would say, "Tell us more!"

OK. I would inform them about other bodily functions like fluid waste. "The average person loses about five pints of liquid a day," the book said.

Here's the breakdown by the author:
"Urine – 2.5 pints
Perspiration – 1.25 pints
Exhaled moisture from lungs – 1 pint
Feces – (about ¾ of fecal matter is water) – .25 pint."

After this information, I gave them a demonstration. Before they arrived I poured apple juice into a vial, so that when the lesson started they did not know they were seeing juice and not urine. I then asked them to pass it around, which of course gave rise to lots of "*eeewwws*!" But they gladly did so, especially the boys who find more interest in bathroom humor than girls, in general. Of course, I eventually let them in on my high jinx, which they had come to expect from me over time.

One year I developed problems from a gallstone. It was actually more than one stone. I researched the situation and tried to avoid surgery as I had already had a caesarian birth and ovarian cyst removal and just didn't want any more cutting. I scheduled several doctor appointments to see if I could avoid going under the knife. I even made an appointment with a Dr. Carter, a urologist in Atlanta, who I had heard invented Shock Wave Lithotripsy (SWL) which is the most common treatment for kidney stones in the United States. I heard you were submerged in a pool of water to have it done. I thought if you can get rid of kidney stones this way, why not *Gall*stones? After our meeting, I found that removing gallstones didn't work that way. I would have to undergo surgery. Lucky for me they had developed a new way to remove gallstones: laparoscopic gallbladder surgery which removes the gallbladder and gallstones through several small incisions in the abdomen. After it was all over, they asked if I would like to keep the stones. I said yes. They gave me a small glass container to store them in.

I decided to use the gallstones to teach a life science lesson. I brought out the enclosed glass container with gallstones one day. Not telling them what was in the glass jar, I just mentioned that I had purchased a few rare stones recently and they really cost me a lot of money. (I really don't remember the cost of the operation in 1998 but it wasn't cheap.) I asked, "Would you like to see them?

Those poor little 7th graders were my captive audience. What were they supposed to say? Of course they wanted to see my rare stones that I told them I had paid big bucks for. So, I whipped the jar out. I handed it to the first person on the front row and they proceeded to pass it from student to student. While they were examining them, I expounded about the stones: how they came from a unique place, that they were very valuable, that I would never have any more, and I wanted to share it with them so they could get a good look at such rare gems, etc.

The gallstones themselves looked like cockleburs: round but with grey/brown spiky points sticking out and not pretty at all, but since they hadn't seen a *stone* like that, they didn't question it. As the last of the students examined the contents of the jar, I told them the relationship to the gemstones and me. That was a great moment, too. Another gross-out!

And, of course, I always told these gross stories right before we'd break for lunch to make it more effective, timing it right down to the minute the lunch bell rang as they gagged while walking to line up for lunch.

The Exorcist

Setting: A 1970s middle class home somewhere in America.

A father and mother are concerned about their only child, David. Their son, an 8th grade honor student, Boy Scout, teacher pleaser, and popular child has become moody and withdrawn in the last few weeks. His grades have dropped. He is no longer interested in his friends. He stays in his room after school until dinner and as soon as his plate is cleared, immediately retreats back to his bedroom, his haven.

His only interest he has is working on a project for his Boy Scouts of America den. He tirelessly gives the project his attention night and day, week in and week out, and it consumes his time on weekends as well. His parents see this involvement with the scouts as the only redeeming factor in his new behavior, so they hope the rest of his demeanor will eventually change again, and soon, for the good.

Teachers are concerned as well. They mentioned to David's parents about his being absent-minded when turning in homework assignments. They see him blankly staring out the classroom windows and not engaging in class discussions no matter what the subject. Loving science and math like he did, he is now listless, lethargic, or lazy. They don't know how to describe their concern. They have a parent conference to inform David's parents about their son. Questions are asked:

"Is David getting enough sleep?"

"Is he depressed?"

"Does it appear he is taking drugs?"

"Is he keeping the same friends he had before or is he hanging out with a new crowd?"

"Is it a phase?"

David's parents pass along these concerns to their son who doesn't seem to be the least bit interested in school. His only concern is getting his project done on time to claim another merit badge. And although this project keeps him busy for a worthy cause, they can't help but take note of what his teachers are uneasy about as well.

Being the faithful Catholics that they are, they pray. A lot. Their anxiety increases as time goes by. They can't help but think about a movie they saw in the theater the year before. Surely not, they think, but could it be? David is now talking back to his parents and is loud. He started having tantrums and breaking things in the house. They notice he wasn't sleeping well as they started hearing his radio on during the early morning hours. Soon after, they heard his incoherent speech, he was delusional, had bizarre muscular ticks, wasn't eating, his eyes looked possessed, and he didn't want to go to school.

All kinds of terrible thoughts went directly back to that movie, *The Exorcist*. They couldn't help but ponder, "Was their own son possessed by the devil like in the movie?" The movie was inspired by the 1971 New York Times Bestseller by William Peter Blatty about a real 1949 exorcism. In the book and movie, a mother attempts to win her twelve-year-old daughter back from the demonic possession with the help of two priests who perform an exorcism.

They set up one for David and soon enough he was back at school where his congenial personality had returned.

They figured out that his new merit badge which he was working on was to blame, as it took him away from his family, school, and friends for hours, days, and weeks with his bedroom door *closed*. His new passion was making model anything – cars, planes, bridges – and it was the glue fumes from these crafts that was the cause of his freakish behavior.

Microeconomics 101

I wasted this great lesson plan on a room full of 6th graders. Or did I? It wasn't a waste, really, except 6th graders don't remember much about middle school and this lesson was an important one. I was conducting an economics exercise.

I took a break from teaching before our second baby was born and sold real estate for John Wieland. If you know his business theory, he builds neighborhood friendly homes around clubhouses, Olympic size swimming pools for swim meets but also with slides for the kiddies, nature trails, etc. His business has/had its own lumber, real estate, interior design, and financing companies all housed under one roof. He sold houses like car dealers sell cars: choose a house plan, then for 'such-and-such' price (which was pre-set), you can have more – like all brick, or a garden tub, maybe a screen porch, or that sunroom. Just tack it on to the base price of the house. Every purchaser is really not so individualistic after all. It's pre-arranged. You can get extra on that base plan– if you pay for it.

What was the point I was making? *A-Real-Life-Wake-Up-Call*.

Remember *Parade* magazine that was a supplement to the *Atlanta Journal Constitution*? Every year they featured on their front page "What People Earn". On that yearly cover, tiny little portraits of about 100 people from every walk of life were featured with their occupation and income. I cut out those pictures, placed males' images in one envelope and females' in another. There were incomes ranging from under $10,000 to over a million. People in the service industry, teachers, postal workers, professional football players, models, car salesmen, dentists…you name it. A variety of people from different ages, backgrounds, colors, and education were all featured.

The male students picked a random person from the male envelope and the females from theirs. I began my lesson: "Here's an average house. And its cost to build on an average lot is '$$.'" I described down payment, private mortgage insurance, homeowners insurance, utilities, etc. I mentioned if they bought a car what monthly payments might be for that also, and I mentioned possible grocery costs.

Then after explaining what all was involved with debt, I randomly picked students to reveal their income from the people they chose from the envelopes. Then I placed a carrot in front of them – another house – this time one with all the bells and whistles.

"I want a garden tub," some would say.

"You can't afford it," I answered to several. "But those with the large incomes can."

"And I want that screen porch!"

"You can't get it. Not with your down payment. If you want to put more down, banks might lower your mortgage. Unless you've saved enough, you won't be able to change the numbers on that."

"But, I *want* it!"

"Yeah, well, maybe if you were married. A dual income changes everything. You probably could afford it then."

Wait a minute. I could see the light bulbs go off in their 12-year-old heads! And then the scrambling started. Boys were chasing the most financially successful girls and girls were trying to catch the most prosperous boys. All over the classroom you heard, "Will you marry me?"

And now the other lesson learned was that these pretend professionals who had either advanced degrees or somehow worked hard toward an end goal of comfortable wealth realized they didn't *need* a partner. Male and female students, because of the luck in their chosen person, actually realized the importance of being profitable enough and what it brought to the playing field. They could do it alone if they wanted. They had a choice.

I do hope their adolescent brains retained something from this.

You've Come A Long Way, Baby!

In my books, I sometimes dole out advice whether you want it or not. There have been tips about Do-It-Yourself-Dentistry but today I am giving you tips on how to have better disciplined young children. Mine are grown. There is nothing more I can really do except let them figure it out for themselves. Some of you still have another option. In the early 1990s, I had been out of education for a decade. Did I really want to go back? I tried my hand at substitute teaching first, you know, the job that doesn't have much respect by students. Their mentality was "How much can we get away with today with this stupid person?" I had four years teaching experience and knew what they were thinking, so I decided to beat them at their own game.

Students' parents signed a waiver giving permission to allow the use of any image of their child for any type of school related media - school calendars, newspaper stories of school events, and any other kind of visuals that might be used in the media promoting the school system, but nothing was said of audio recordings. So, at every middle or high school I walked in to 'babysit' that day, I first stopped by the media center, asked for a tape recorder and blank cassette tape, walked confidently toward the classroom with both, and set the recorder at the front of the classroom for all to see. When the bell rang to start class, before I took roll, I proceeded to tell the class the reason for the recording device: I was going to audio record their voices and behavior that day and give it to their teacher along with my notes about this particular class.

After that announcement, *in front of the entire class*, I pushed the record/play buttons at the same time to start the process...and I pushed them with grandeur to dramatize the moment so they were aware that their behavior was being monitored starting at that point. Everything was transparent. At the end of the day, I placed my notes and the cassette in the teacher's box so she would have it immediately when she checked for an update of how things went when she was absent. She could *hear* how it went.

Believe me, it worked. Sometimes when the class was a little rowdy, I called down a student or two, first, with their voices being captured on the recording and then second, with their names, as the teacher might have heard, "Abigail? Settle down a bit." One time when the behavior was recorded, it enhanced a case about a student who was disruptive with his regular teacher, also. And that was good ammunition for her to discipline that pupil.

I tell mothers today about how they can keep their children in line either at home or just as importantly – *in public*! Wish I could have taken my own advice. My boys are thirty-three and twenty-five. In this eight-year-age-difference there were inventions that did improve my mothering capabilities from the oldest to the youngest. But what I needed most hadn't been invented yet...the photo/video options of the cell phone.

Why did I need this particular phone function and what do I tell mothers today about *why* they should utilize this photo/video recording on their own children? Because when children, like my own did at times, start acting out - *record* it. There really is no discussion later when you disagree over the behavior you wanted changed. The child (I think you could do this step even as young as three?) sees his/her action that you want thwarted and instead of "intentionally not remembering" or "*really* not remembering", the incident is captured to hone in on the behavior you want improved.

You're welcome.

Testing, Testing

I have always worked in counties that had the block schedule in middle and high school.
That means the school calendar is divided into 2 semesters or blocks of 18 weeks. One semester ends with final exams before the Christmas break. When we come back from that break, the second half of the year begins.

No one looks forward to tests – students (because they have to take them) or teachers (because they have to grade them). Being an English teacher is not easy when it comes to grading. Essays, remember? I used to jokingly say, "I wonder if the more wine I drink while grading these essays if their grades will improve?"

Another hardship on an English teacher during the year and especially at mid-term testing was the copying machine that would break down at the most inopportune time. It just didn't break down for an hour. Sometimes it was days. Somebody had to call the company to send someone out to fix it and fixing it took all day, for some reason. Machine parts were all over the floor during the operation. One couldn't wait to see the taped sign that said, "*Not working*!" taken off the top of the machine. By the time it was removed, there was mold on it.

Before the copier, we used the mimeograph machine (often abbreviated to mimeo) and it was a low-cost duplicating machine that worked by forcing ink through a stencil onto paper. I loved the smell of that ink running through it. Not for long lengths of time, though. I heard one could get high from the smell by the overuse of the machine. I used to jokingly say, "I wonder if I smell more of this purple ink while running off these tests if their grades will improve?"

Did I mention the joys of bathroom duty? My pre-21st century schools had teachers rotate bathroom duty assignments. I could never, *ever* eat my lunch in the girls' restroom during duty time like one teacher I know who made it a regular practice. She scooted a desk in there and plopped her cafeteria tray on top of it and dug in. Isn't that awful?

Another one of my teacher girlfriends left teaching public school and was hired at The Westminster Schools in Atlanta. She and I kept in touch and she reported to me that she still had bathroom duty. She was also assigned bus duty, too, but not for the obvious reasons of keeping order: there were many kids with million-dollar-last-names who were enrolled and the school didn't want any of their students kidnapped.

I Am A Sucker!

I am a sucker for all those tests that show up online, mostly on Facebook, that can tell your Intellectual Quotient, your Emotional Quotient, your aura color, your top personality traits, which movie star you look like, what literary character you are most like, etc., all in ten to twenty questions. I'm a S-U-C-K-E-R.

I have the highest Facebook IQ, the most tenderhearted EQ, every color of the rainbow when I retake that color test for the tenth time to get a color I want because I answer the questions differently each time trying to score my favorite color, such a great personality I should run for office, am Grace Kelly's doppelganger, a Scarlett O'Hara literary heroine, and can score 20 on a scale of 1-10. I might as well be a Barbie Doll because she's so perfect.

Barbie is found with many careers from a model to a surgeon. She is vintage, but yet fashionable. She dresses for all the holidays and still wears a spacesuit. She is thin and yet can be curvy. She is every ethnicity. She is the darling of the seas as Ariel or she can fly on a magic carpet like Jasmine. She is expensive but also frugal. She wears designer Mattel clothes but also wears homemade frocks from Amazon, Etsy, or your favorite seamstress. She is a collector but some throw her away after her hair tangles. She might like to have a boyfriend but doesn't need one. And she has a fast pink convertible. This girl rocks.

According to my online tests I am as fantastic as she.

And it only took a minute to answer all the questions because they were all multiple choice.

You know about multiple-choice tests, don't you? They "consist of a stem, the correct answer, keyed alternative, and distractors. The stem is the beginning part of the item that presents the item as a problem to be solved, a question asked of the respondent, or an incomplete statement to be completed, as well as any other relevant information." 1

Middle schools gave 'aptitude' tests. The counselors administered these tests to gain insight into the kinds of jobs/careers students could be thinking about for their future. They gave these tests before high school so that pupils could plan on what courses they should take for either the college-prep course track diploma or the technical-track diploma.

The test was absolutely correct when it came to my first child's innate ability. The outcome indicated he was good with his hands. The test suggested he become an air conditioning repairman or a butcher. He is now Director for the Learning Environments of labs, classroom, and collaborative spaces for Georgia State University. Fancy name for he works in IT and uses his hands.

But I think what I worry a little about is the girl who sat next to him in his eighth grade classroom. When the results came in, she told our oldest child her test results. I wonder what she is doing today. Her test results told her she should either become a clown... or a mime.

A Day in the Life of a Teacher

Middle School Version

Going to school was always an adventure, never knowing what I was going to be asked to do outside of teaching *my* students on any given day. I had a reading specialist certificate add-on to my state middle school certificate. The state education department was promoting reading under a new administration. Teachers were required to share part of their day to help students improve their reading skills. With my reading certificate, I was assigned an entire class of remedial eighth graders who were reading on the third grade level.

I heard their complaints every day because they despised picture books and really wanted to 'read' chapter books. These kids could read the words but they just could not comprehend *what* they had read.

As I walked down the hall toward my room, I am continually reminded of how middle school students' brains work. There is a poster near my classroom door created by some middle school club with good intentions raising awareness for a good cause but it read: <u>Child Abuse Week</u>, not *Prevent* Child Abuse Week.

Georgia schools initiated the TAPProgram – the Georgia Teacher Alternative Preparation Program allowing certification of individuals who held a bachelor's degree or higher from an accredited institution but who did not complete a teacher education program but wanted to transition to the teaching profession. Our health teacher had to leave for an emergency one day and the office was not able to find a substitute to cover for her. They asked around if teachers would give up their planning period to take over one of her health classes. I offered because if this happened to me, it would be comforting to know someone was looking out for me, too.

With no permanent classroom because health and physical education was divided with nine weeks for health and nine weeks for P.E., she was not assigned a permanent classroom for so short a time on the health curriculum. The health teacher was always assigned another teacher's empty classroom during that particular teacher's planning period. So, this meant, I had to go where the students were already assigned to meet. Sometimes the teachers who offered their classrooms for the health classes chose to remain in the classroom during the health lessons while others chose to leave.

The day I was called to substitute for the physical education/health teacher and she was to use a TAPP teacher's classroom. This novice educator, oddly enough, always chose to remain in the room, probably to gain classroom management skills as a newbie. While I was presenting the assignment that day, she began raising her hand and asking questions as if she were one of the students!

Walking back to my own seventh grade life science classroom after covering the health class, I passed by another science teacher's lab and I saw her notes on cell structure on her white board. Life sciences explore the origins, evolution, and expansion of life in all its forms. The students looked really involved in their study. They were viewing several slides on genetics that day.

As I passed the lab, I heard one student shout out, "I have an orgasm (organism) on my slide!"

I needed to share this with one of my teacher friends who I saw in the hall between classes. Having a moment to retell what I overheard, she said she was having a rough day, too. She was a sixth grade social studies teacher whose pupils were studying Ancient Greece. She and her co-teacher divided them into groups so they could collaborate on their Greek projects that they were overseeing. To differentiate the groups, she mentioned the kids had been driving them crazy because it was almost time for spring break and they were already wild.

To help them through their last days before the spring break, these co-teachers planned a little fun for themselves without the students' knowledge. They gave the groups color names but while most well-behaved students who were working hard on their group projects received names as red, blue, yellow, and orange, the worst behaved group was assigned the color, puce.

While the groups were given colors, the individual students received Greek sounding names and those whose behaviors were totally offensive received offensive sounding Greek names, like a boy who farted so much after lunch was given the name Pootacles. A female student who was always bugging her team was named Obnoxia. And still, another female who was a real pain was assigned Dyspepsia. Of course the students never knew.

My last class of the day ended with another reading assignment. One of the books that we read together was about Robin Hood and naturally Sherwood Forest was mentioned. In the community where I worked there was a Putt-Putt golf course called Sherwood Forest. As there was a picture in our book of a huge redwood tree, one of my students was infuriated. She got up from her desk with book in hand, and pointed to the tree. She loudly stated that there was no such tree at Sherwood Forest because she had just been there over the weekend and didn't see it.

But my day wasn't over yet. After school, I volunteered to help regular classroom teachers with in-coming student permanent record folders that were being transferred from fifth-grade teachers in elementary school to sixth-grade teachers in middle school for the coming year. These folders had color-coded tag information on them, i.e.: female, male, high achiever, slow learner, Caucasian, African-American, Hispanic, Disability, No Disability, Other, etc. This was done to keep teachers from having to read through every student's file to compose diversity in the classroom. As a support teacher, I was helping homeroom teachers create their classrooms for the next school year. I didn't know all the colors for the categories but they were pastel like a rainbow. One color stood out. It was fire-engine red. I asked about the tag color and what it meant. A general classroom teacher told me that those tags were for "disagreeable parents."

Glad that day was over. But what will tomorrow bring?

High School

"F" - Failure or Fantastic? You Decide

When I was in pre-school (over sixty years ago) I had this creative teacher whose own children were ingenious. One of her brood ended up at MIT and discovered another part of the atom. I once heard that when he was in first grade, he received an "F" on a report card. When he brought this information home, he asked his mother, "What does 'F' mean?" She remarked, "It means you are *fantastic*!" She couldn't bring herself to tell him what it really meant because, after all, he was just six.

I have a long resume of teaching gigs: church preschool, church adult Sunday School, public elementary school, homeschool, public middle school, public high school, public summer school, and public night school. My night school job was an eye-opening one. Thank goodness for this last chance at gaining an education for some students. Those who make the most of it, I congratulate you! But for those who are not attending to get ahead, please don't disrupt me
while I am trying to teach you something. Are you showing up just to be able to get a driver's license? Let's learn something new!

I was informed later that I had a female student who was in my night school class because she was tossed out of her former county school system because she threw a desk at someone. A *desk*! I think that someone was a teacher. My county hadn't given us training on desk dodging yet. I tried to make these American Literature lessons relevant. I really did. One student obediently came to class every night, sat quiet as a mouse, and yet failed every test. When he didn't pass the class he spoke to me for the first time (although I did try to prompt him to contribute to the discussion in class to little success).

He asked me why he made an "F". I answered that 1) he made an "F" on every test and 2) there was not much contribution from him in the class discussions for me to be able to determine if he had absorbed the material sufficiently to pass. I couldn't tell what he had learned. He responded, "But I came to class every night!"

I countered by saying, "Would I use a doctor that showed up to my surgery with a *scalpel* making "F's" on all his grades just because he attended every medical lecture? Would
you want that?"

He was a really nice guy and I hated to drop that bombshell on him, but I certainly couldn't *give* him something without some signs of comprehension. It wouldn't be fair to those who did work for it. I felt terrible for him.

Gosh, it's hard on the students these days. I am not being sarcastic either. It really is. All the demands they and others put on themselves. They need to remember this: more "C" average college students become CEO's of corporations. They have learned how to balance fun and grades.

My good friend, Swoozie, worked for a public school test prep company whose website's mission statement read:

PRACTICE MAKES PERFECT

With lots of opportunities to review and practice concepts and skills, Common Core Performance

Coach is the program that will pave the path to success on the new high-stakes assessments. The program allows teachers to implement lessons in a variety of ways and can reinforce Common Core Coach instruction or supplement any other program. Many examples are provided in order to solidify understanding. Practice tests mirror question types that will be seen in the new assessments and simulates in paper format what students will see online. Common Core Performance Coach is perfect for ongoing instruction throughout the year or more intensive instruction and test prep before the tests.

She once received a phone call while at work. The name that popped up on her phone screen read, *Jesus* (she was nervous for a moment that *Jesus* was calling - *lol)*. Well, after rationalizing, and coming to that conclusion, she answered and heard, "Can I speak to the manager?" She said the caller sounded very young. She replied, "I'm the manager. How can I help?" He commented, "I'm in class right now and I need the answers."

She replied, "I am sorry but we don't provide answers to students." He said, "Thank you" and hung up. Using his cell phone in class, he must have found her company's website and called for *the test answers!*

Some things change: He was so polite…and I bet he showed up every day to class but still couldn't pass a test to save his life.

Take Me Out to the Ballgame

Some may argue that baseball is still America's 'National Pastime' because recent polls see a surge in football. Yet, Ken Burns has produced a documentary for PBS on baseball, so it *must* still be at the top. As I've pointed out in several stories, my dad was a pretty good ballplayer. In high school he was on, what I'd call, a traveling team, because this story took place in the spring of 1932 when my father was seventeen years old and his team competed with anybody and everybody that hosted a game. So, in the late spring of 1932 these ball players were in Atlanta playing some of the guards at the Atlanta Penitentiary while a few of the inmates were allowed to watch.

My dad, a left-handed pitcher, who not only received an athletic college scholarship but also received a professional contract, was playing in the outfield during this particular game. While playing centerfield, he kept stepping farther and farther back…just a little at a time so as to not draw attention while doing so. He kept inching backwards because he saw two men sitting on some bleachers and he wanted to ask them a question. He had heard there was a certain high profile inmate at the Atlanta Pen and he wanted to find out if it was true. So, little by little he meandered towards the bleachers getting close enough to eventually turn around and ask if this infamous person was indeed incarcerated there.

Was this American gangster, the reputed boss of the Chicago Outfit and famous Prohibition era ruffian really there? Was this crime boss whose seven-year reign of smuggling and bootlegging liquor in the building? Was this man, in a league of his own, who terrorized Chicago during Prohibition in the 1920s, and who was convicted of tax evasion in 1931 an inmate in Atlanta's prison?

This gangster was sent to the Atlanta U.S. Penitentiary in May 1932. At 250 pounds he was officially diagnosed with syphilis and gonorrhea. He also suffered from withdrawal symptoms from cocaine addiction. He was competent at his prison job of stitching the soles on shoes for eight hours a day, yet he was barely coherent when writing his letters. At the Atlanta Pen he was seen as a weak personality and was *not* the mobster from which his legend was derived. He was so out of his depth dealing with the bullying his fellow inmates inflicted that his cellmate feared that this thug would have a nervous breakdown.

His cellmate, Red Rudinsky, was formerly a small time criminal associated with this racketeer and saw himself as a protector for this notorious hooligan. With this conspicuous protection from Rudinsky and a few others, prisoners drew accusations and fueled suspicion from less friendly inmates that this infamous inmate was receiving special treatment. There was never any solid evidence but it became part of the rationale for moving this notorious man to the recently opened Alcatraz Federal Penitentiary off the coast of San Francisco.

My high-school-aged dad was very curious. Was he still there? Still backing his way farther into the outfield and not wanting it to seem that he was not paying attention to the game and his position, my gangly seventeen-year-old father was close enough now to swivel around to find his answer. He quickly asked these two men sitting there watching the game if Alphonse Gabriel "Al" Capone was in the Atlanta Penitentiary?

One of the two answered, "He sure is, and he's sitting right here next to me."

CYA

I taught every grade except second grade. I even taught in my church sponsored pre-school program. When I received my gifted certification, I was able to teach elementary, middle, and high school. While teaching 9th grade gifted English, I got the wind knocked out of me a bit one day when my assistant principal just walked into my classroom *unannounced*, interrupted my class lesson, asked me *in front of all my students* to please see him in his office at the end of my class, and left.

Now, this did not look good. And it didn't help that my students snickered because it appeared as though their teacher was about to be reprimanded. But I had a feeling I knew what this was going to be about. And I was prepared. Feeling a little more composed, I walked into his office and there sat *another* assistant principal, who was in charge of curriculum and instruction. Uh, oh. I may have been in bigger trouble than I thought.

I was asked to sit down in a chair in front of his desk. There were two chairs there. The curriculum and instruction department assistant was in the other chair. The AP who had called the meeting began...

"Mrs. St. John, a mother called to inform us about her concern regarding her son who is in your class. She was washing his clothes and as she cleaned out his pants pockets, she came upon a note. The note was from her son to another student which hadn't been delivered yet but she was worried about the content of this note and turned it over to us to get to the bottom of it."

"Well, sure. What did it say?"

The AP continued, "Let me read the note to you and then you can respond, OK?"

"OK," I squeaked as I started to sweat.

The note read, "Hey, dude. What's up? I am in my English class right now. What are you doing? Mrs. St. John is so cool. She flips birds, she cusses, and she is showing us nudity in a movie."

Busted!

But all of it was true and I had a good excuse. I began, "In 9th grade we read, Shakespeare's *Romeo and Juliet*, and in Act I, scene 1, there are comments by those loyal to both the Montagues (Romeo's family) and the Capulets (Juliet's family) in the street of Verona regarding how they feel about each other and their kin. There has been a long-standing feud between the two families."

I looked over at the curriculum and instruction assistant principal and she nodded her head in agreement.

I continued, "And in that scene, they chide each other by asking back and forth, 'Do you bite your thumb, sir?' says one.

'Yes, I bite my thumb sir,' says the other.

'Do you bite your thumb at me, sir?'

'Yes, I do bite my thumb, sir, but not at you.'

And so my students asked me, 'What does that mean, Mrs. St. John?'

I had to give it straight to these two educators. So, I added, "And you know what I said? 'Oh, come on! Don't you really know? It's like flipping the bird.' Of course, I did *not* flip one, but I came close. I did demonstrate the action of my right arm bent with a raised fist and the slap of the left hand on the right upper arm. Boom!"

"So," the AP said looking at the instructional assistant principal, "That study is in our approved curriculum?"

"Yes, it is," she answered as she nodded.

"Mrs. St. John, what about the cussing?" my supervisor questioned.

I answered, *Night* by Elie Wiesel has many quotes using expletives. Wiesel wrote about his experiences in Auschwitz and Buchenwald with his father, the Nazi German concentration camps in 1944 – 1945 at the height of the Holocaust toward the end of World War II. When I read aloud and came to the lines that say 'sons of bitches' or other obscenities, quoting directly from the book, I certainly don't change anything. I read exactly what he wrote."

He again acquiesced to the other AP, "Is that part of the 9th grade curriculum?"

"It is," she responded.

Now that was two accusations down with one to go. "So, let's see now. Oh, yes. The mother mentioned nudity. How do you explain that?"

"Well, the Franco Zeffirelli's movie version of *Romeo and Juliet* (a 1968 film that I even saw when I was in the 9th grade in 1968) is not rated. It has been approved by the county and when we finish the play, I show it."

"She's correct," said the other assistant principal.

I went on, "And in this movie, there is this tiny little scene where Juliet and Romeo consummate their marriage which shows Romeo's rompus pompos. There was no frontal nudity and no more than 5 seconds of his buttocks in plain view."

"Well, Mrs. St. John, let's skip over that naked behinny scene the next time perhaps," he suggested.

And with that, my meeting was over. Thank goodness for the little things in life. I continued to cuss and flip birds in class. I even continued to show that nude scene because whenever I attempted to fast forward that part of the movie with my remote control, *for some odd reason*, the TV remote failed to work...*every time*! ☺

KD - The Gift That Keeps On Giving

I *am* a Kappa Delta.

Who would have thought being song leader for my chapter at Georgia Southern University in 1973 would prove so valuable when I started teaching gifted 9th grade English in 2006? Since I am a tactile person, my philosophy had always been to incorporate as many of the senses in my lesson plans to reach all the different learning styles. Maybe something will hit home.

And it did.

"The Odyssey" is required reading in our county's 9th grade English curriculum. Because of the Greek setting, every year I would tell my students that I could sing the Greek alphabet. What a talent. Hoping to take away from class instruction, students always begged me to sing it. Of course I did. It was in my repertoire, they just didn't know it. They were impressed. But the ham I am, I kept going.

Would they like to hear me sing some more Greek songs? "Of course!" they urged. "Take all the time you need until the bell rings! This is different!" Because I was affiliated with music (from piano to voice) from childhood, I remembered the Greek songs from the other sororities when I went through rush.

"Pi, Pi, ADPi, like 'em, love 'em, 'til I die…"
"Well, I'm a Zeta (pause) Zeta (pause), Zeta, Zeta, Z-T-A."
"Phi Mu, Phi Mu, Phi Mu Fraternity, Phi Mu, Phi Mu, Phi Mu for me."

NOW I have their undivided attention.
"More! More!" they shouted.

"With a K, with a K, with a Kaa, and P, and P, and Ppa, Kappa Delta!

Love 'em, love 'em, love 'em, love 'em, love 'em 'til you die.

Come KD's, come on KD's, lift your spirits high!

All the KD's love to sing and shout, HEY!: With a K…"(repeat first line)

But their favorite was:

"I'm a KD Lady,
I'm a red-hot baby,
I'm the hottest thing in town.
And when it comes to lovin',
I'm a human oven,
I can burn you right down to the ground."

And with that last line, I'd take my thumb, lick it, shake it in the air, and say "psssst."
("psssst" is an onomatopoeia for those who remember their literary terms – just had to throw that in there to show that I can not only tie in Greek songs to my lessons, but literary terms as well. LOL)

Now they are hootin', hollerin', and clapping! They may not remember what *The Odyssey* was about but they'll never forget it, I hoped.

Fast-forward four years. One of those precious students in that classroom is now graduating from high school. She told her mother, my neighbor, that she wants to be a Kappa Delta at the University of Georgia. I am totally excited. I write her recommendation and she pledges! I never made friends on Facebook with former students until they graduated. And since that class of 2010 moved out of the building, I could.

Finding out that she was not only my darling former student but also going to be my sister, I made her a KD scrapbook to collect all her sorority memorabilia during her future activities that she was going to have while being KD at UGA. Her mother later told me how much she treasured it and how packed it became.

But after learning about this news of her pledging, I posted on Facebook that this student was going to be a KD and how proud I was. I heard back from another student from her graduating class who was in my room that day of my performance and she wrote on my Facebook wall, "Well, of course! Not only is she a KD Lady but she is also red hot baby!"

These students were fourteen or fifteen years old when I sang that song. They were now eighteen or nineteen and that one sweet former student wrote back about remembering that particular moment.

No Kappa Delta *was* a Kappa Delta. We a*re* still Kappa Deltas. Although, I am sure by retelling this story, I am now an embarrassment to my chapter.

What Were You Expecting?

Dear Teachers,

Welcome back to school. Some of you are teaching for the first time. It's overwhelming to be a new teacher and being held responsible. There is soooooo much you have to be accountable for these days. What's the saying? "Being a teacher is like having 1,234 tabs open on your computer." Ain't it the truth? You are all things to everybody.

In 1979, I remember I was anxious those few days in my first high school job. I adorned my room with all kinds of posters pertaining to the authors that I was about to teach. There were grammar rules on signs on the walls as reminders, too. It *looked* like I knew what I was doing teaching high school English. Well, I really did know my curriculum, but the students knew I was raw. They planned an attack on their unassuming teacher who was only about six years older than they were. Let's call it *The Incident*.

I had been teaching a little over a month and all seemed fine. The students and I got along well. They were well behaved. I was happy. But, the day before *The Incident*, I left school without deleting my notes from the chalkboard. There was a lot of information from my lesson but I had to leave fast to catch my carpool ride home with another single female teacher. In 1979 our rooms consisted of a grey or green slate board, with white chalk, and dusty grey chalk erasers made of felt. Today there are dry erase boards, with dry erase markers (in wonderful colors, too), and dry erasers. No chalk dust anywhere.

Since I left in a hurry the day before, I arrived in homeroom to find my notes still visible. Since I was presenting new information to the students for first period, the board had to be completely erased, so as I wiped the eraser across the board, and there was a *whish* sound and a streak of fire lit up in front of my face! It was just as quick and bright as lightning! These absolutely clever, funny, creative, but would-they-get-in-big-trouble-10th-grade-pupils pulled this prank by placing long matches in the creases of the eraser. When I brushed it across the board, the slate and matches connected and it lit up for a few seconds like sparklers in front of my face.

Then… nothing but silence.

I turned around. Eyeball to eyeball I looked at every student who was in my homeroom that morning. Some were sitting in their desks. Others were standing up watching and waiting for my reaction. I was in disbelief. They were quietly anticipating *some* kind of penalty to be handed out at any moment. And after this pause and with them looking like deer in headlights, I said, "That was great!"

That was *not* the response they were expecting from me. Yet, I did not send one student to the office to be reprimanded.

Sincerely,

Lee (We Got Away With It) St. John

F***

Daddy played sports his whole life. He was the first person in our town and surrounding area to win an athletic scholarship and was offered one in baseball to Atlanta's Oglethorpe University. It was a school that had a fantastic baseball team. He also played basketball. They played powerhouse teams in those days – the University of Georgia and Georgia Tech, among others. My dad was a pitcher. He was what one called a "Lefty" or "Southpaw". He also wrote with his left hand but played golf with his right. Ambidextrous, I guess.

Daddy left Oglethorpe University before graduation to play pro baseball for the Chicago Cubs. When World War II broke out, his promising baseball career was cut short. He married my mother during the war and when it was over, he went back to Oglethorpe to finish his degree. He gave up his dream of playing major league baseball because the pay was measly (even for the Cubs) and he needed to make a financially stable life for a wife and future family, yet, he still loved the game.

He loved it so much that, after he graduated from college, he became the first coach hired for the county high school. Not only was he the first coach, but he was also the *only* coach. Not only was he the *only* coach for football, he was also the *only* coach for every other sport at the school. He managed them all. I guess he was the school's athletic director. After several years and needing more income than that of a high school teacher/mentor, he left coaching and education behind. But those who still wanted "Coach" around asked him to announce the football games on the public address system for the football team during their season. He knew the rules of the game backward and forward, in and out, and would be able to still be a part of the high school football team atmosphere. Daddy took the job and received a little extra pay for it.

My dad once told this story: our region 1A school in the 1950s didn't have much in the way of a PA system like many of the densely student populated schools with grander stadiums and press boxes. The press box Daddy used had a wooden light pole with wooden steps nailed to it so that he could climb up into a teeny-tiny-tree-house-looking platform with a sound system, which was probably less than 16 square feet. He called all the home games from that public address box.

Over the summer from one season to the next, the wood box on the pole wasn't used for anything. I guess someone rigged up the system every fall for calling games and made sure the wood slats were stable enough to climb. September in the South back in the 1950s and 1960s seemed to be much colder then. Daddy bundled up and climbed up into the little "press" box, turned on the public address system, and when he was ready to test the PA system…as they say, "all hell broke loose."

Families – young and old – seated for the game, snuggled up in their blankets and holding their hot chocolate in paper cups heard it: every single 4-letter word imaginable blared from the sound system. Just like in "A Christmas Story" television movie when Ralphie's father uttered all his cuss words clanging on the boiler, the same words passed my father's lips.

"F***!!!   SH**!!!   Damn-it!!!   What the hell?"

Wasps had made a nest inside the call box from the previous season and my dad was highly allergic. He flailed his arms while trying to protect himself from the dangerous venom. He did not realize the sound system was turned *on*. Parents covered their children's ears. It was embarrassing. And legend has it that his ranting, raving, and cussing voice was even heard the next county over. What a way to make an impression as an announcer during the first game of the season.

Student Teaching: Who is Teaching Whom?

Before actually teaching, college students studying to become teachers not only have their own education courses to learn but also they get the field experience of teaching in a classroom with a seasoned supervising teacher. Student teaching is like trying it out to see if you actually want to continue with a degree in education. One of my girlfriends found out that particular role was not for her and she took another avenue – she became a flight attendant for a major airline.

I liked being with the older students. I felt like they were very relatable as I was only about six years older than the students I was assigned. My mother taught high school and I was always hanging around with the high school students from an early age and it was my second home because Mother was sponsoring this or that and I would hang out with her after school when I was younger.

But I had a label that dwarfed me: I was a *student* teacher. My sponsoring teacher must have thought I was handling things pretty well and let me direct the students at times without her always micromanaging me while observing my teaching lessons or technique. I tried to also be professional looking, but I didn't have money to buy a professional wardrobe to pull that off. I guess I did wear what was in my closet and for a twenty-three year old it wasn't matronly. And at 5'5 ½" I might have looked like one of their own. That was another disadvantage. Did I know my subject matter? I did, but they weren't listening, really, in this particular high school class because this true event happened in an elective class that was not needed for a Carnegie unit. I was assigned to student teach during Spring Quarter where these particular college bound students had already been accepted to the university of their choice in the fall. And it was the last period of the day. Oh, and my supervising teacher let me have a go at it all by myself.

So, let's review this scenario:

1) It is Spring Quarter.

2) Students are Seniors.

3) I am teaching an elective class that no one needs for graduation, which is just a few weeks away.

4) No supervising educator in the classroom.

5) Mostly males.

6) I am about 6 years older than these pupils.

7) I wear outfits appropriate for my age, not the faculty's age.

8) Last class of the school day.

Got the picture?

One rather oversized male pupil made it a point every day to sit on the first row directly in front of my lectern – just a skinny pole that held a slanted tabletop. Oh, and I sat on a stool while teaching. This guy blabbered and laughed his way in response to everything I did, said, or tried to teach. Whatever words of wisdom came out of my mouth, shortly after, he would mumble some remark that was inaudible to me but not to his classmates. It was funny, I guess, because they laughed. A lot. He slobbered syllables after every teaching point I made. I had to do something to keep my composure and make sure he understood that I was *The Alpha* in this situation so...I took my pointing finger, leaned far over the lectern, gritted my teeth, narrowed my eyes, and I pointed that finger directly at him. With every fiber of my being, I forcefully growled with a loud, intense voice that I didn't even recognize and roared, "*You see me after class !!!!!!!!!*"

And with a Cheshire cat grin, he looked up at me and said, "I'd love to."

I'd leave it there but I have told this story so many times that my listeners have asked, "What did you do?" I'll tell you what I did. I started laughing so hard that the composure I was trying to keep was gone. There was no way I was going to get them back on track after that. So, I said, "Class dismissed."

I have no idea where they went.

The Scarlet Letter Rap

I better be glad I wasn't called into my principal's office for this one.

I taught American Literature in 1999 and believed that grades should be weighted as such: 25% for class participation, 25% for pop quizzes, 25% for major tests, and 25% for projects. I graded this way because I felt it balanced the students' talents. Some students were stronger in speaking skills, some were better with small tests, some better with big tests, and others showed their understanding through other creative means.

While this 11th grade class read, *The Scarlet Letter*, which by the way was an important piece of American Literature written by one of my favorite authors, they thought it archaic and dry. I wanted them to make sure they understood the development of the story, the themes, and symbolism, etc. The students needed to show that they had digested the material and could respond, *within my guidelines*, an expression of that understanding. I tried to make Nathaniel Hawthorne, the author, come alive. He was quite a handsome dude, in my opinion. I loved 19th century American Literature because that's when prose and poetry finally became creative in America. The century before had really been parched and dusty: I mean, letters, sermons, diaries. Where was the fun in reading that?

But in the 19th century you could find Irving, James Fenimore Cooper, Emerson, Longfellow, Poe, Stowe, Frederick Douglas, Whitman, Holmes, Dickinson, Alcott, and Twain, just to name several. When we moved on to the 20th century and its roaring 1920s, we read *The Great Gatsby* by F. Scott Fitzgerald. To make that lesson more fun, I brought the decade to life by having them learn to dance, "The Charleston". I found an old Bennie Goodman LP (which stands for 'long playing'), borrowed a record player from my school's media center, and gave them a few steps to recreate. That dance was a participation grade...not how well they danced, but the fact they *tried* – what an easy grade! I used all kinds of audio, like music, to enhance lessons as much as I could.

That was why I was happy that some of my students decided to write a song, which was on my project list, for *The Scarlet Letter* lesson. The novel, written in the 19th century, began in Boston, Massachusetts in 1642. The plot began with an unmarried woman (and her newborn), who was sentenced in her Puritan community to a punishment for adultery. I recommend reading it since it is a classic. My students were allowed to work in groups for their project. To be fair, I also had them assign a grade for the individuals in their group *in secret* because we all know that some work harder than others in a collaborative setting. You know the rule, "Twenty percent do eighty percent of the work, and eighty percent only do twenty percent of the work."

It was delivery day. There were about 20 project ideas to choose among. A clever group of 17-year-old-boys started in on their song. I was impressed with the choice that these boys made, who I didn't know could sing or were musicians of some sort. In 1999 a very popular song had been on the radio by the band, Smash Mouth. These were the lyrics of the original song:

"Hey, now.
You're an all-star,

Get your game on.
Go. Play.
Hey, now,
You're a rock star,
Get your show on.
Hey, now.
Get paid."

And this was what they created:

"Hey, now,
You're a 'hoe' now…"

I about fell out of my chair.
I bet you wonder what grade they received.

Faking It

John Donne, who I'm sure was one of your favorite poets from your favorite subject, British Literature, in high school wrote what was called metaphysical poetry. This poetry was characterized by the use of metaphysical conceits (unusual surprise comparisons) and paradoxes (a statement that seems to contradict but actually tells the truth). Still with me? It gets better.

In 1999, while teaching "A Valediction: Forbidding Mourning" (I'm sure you remember it) to my 12th grade British Literature class, I was not really happy about having to be enthusiastic about this dumb poem. Yes, I said it...*D-U-M-B* poem. Donne compared *in detail* how two lovers were like a drafting compass. This qualified as a metaphysical poem. English writers during this time were into the metaphysical because of all apparatuses being invented. So he used conceits and paradoxes to get his point across. I had to teach these literary terms and this was the example in our British Literature books. Stay with me. Let's just get this over with. The punch line is great.

His compass was just like the ones you are familiar with – usually made of metal, consisting of two parts connected by a hinge, which can be adjusted. As Wikipedia states, "Typically one part has a spike at its end, and the other part a pencil or sometimes a pen. Circles can be made by fastening one leg of the compass into the paper with the spike, putting the pencil on the paper, and moving the pencil around while keeping the hinge on the same angle. The radius of the circle can be adjusted by changing the angle of the hinge."

Got it? Okay, now you are up to date.

This poem suggested the lovers were like a compass but when I started to use my dad's old compass for show and tell it seemed too small to demonstrate the point to the all the students in the classroom, so…wait for it…

I decided to become the apparatus myself. I stood in the front of the class. My body stood straight with my arms above my head and with my hands touching together like a Vriksasana yoga pose without the leg resting on a knee. I demonstrated *how* the compass was like the lovers by keeping one leg still vertical on the ground as though it was the spike leg of the compass, and by swinging out my right leg, it would exemplify the pencil/pen segment.

I said, "This straight part is like the woman who represents hearth and home (and I think I also said, "Apple Pie and Chevrolet" like the old Chevy commercials when they wanted to present an image of what a perfect home was like) and the man," I continued, "leaves the home as a hunter and gatherer." I swung my right leg out even further and swung it around like the pencil part of the instrument. Imagine this: straight left leg, swirling circles with right leg, and hands fastened together above my head. All this would equal? Yes, you've got it! A compass.

I proceeded with this motion several times: left leg straight and secure on the ground while right leg circled around and around. With this motion, there could be no doubt that I was indeed showing the movement of a drafting compass. Hands clutched together representing souls (and above my head like the souls were higher than everything else in their love – hey, I can make up stuff, too.) Man – hunter and gatherer. Woman – hearth and home. Over and over the hinge held them together as both souls sought to look after the other.

And I thought, "This is crap."

I asked the students, "Do you like this poem?" Some nodded "yes".

"Do you think that I presented it to you in an interesting way so you will remember this poem?" They *all* nodded "yes" to this question.

And now here it comes: I slapped them with, "This is the most stupid poem I have ever read. Do you think I like getting up here making stupid things interesting? Do you think I woke up this morning telling myself, 'Hooray! I get to teach the compass poem today!' Well, I didn't! And what I want to say to you now is that if *I can get up and act like I like being here in front of class teaching a poem I am not particularly fond of...then you can act like you like being here and listening to this...!!!"*

I must say, that was the bigger lesson learned.

Center of Attention

My mother taught school for thirty-seven years before retiring in 1972. She loved being a teacher. She was thirty years old before she married. Born in 1913, she was one of a few women in her generation who even attended college. More remarkably, she also obtained her Master's in Education. She attended Emory University and the University of Georgia. In those very early years of education, one just obtained a teaching certificate and taught any grade level. With her first job, she taught elementary school. She ended her career in high school by teaching American and World Government, a required course for graduation that, at that time, was taught in 12th grade.

Her entire career was spent in one county in Georgia. She began her calling in 1935. One funny story happened early in her career teaching high school. If you know your Georgia history, you know that school used to only be in session eight months of the year, not nine. The school calendar was based around the agricultural summer season where most children were needed at home on their parents' farms. My county, twenty-five-plus miles outside of Atlanta, was very rural. One day in the middle of a classroom lesson, one of her high school students jumped two stories from her open window and left. He went home to work. I guess he figured the farm was more appealing than sitting in a non-air-conditioned classroom learning government. I bet that boy developed a red-neck working outside in that hot Georgia sun.

My mother was adored by her students. She taught for so long and with such loving enthusiasm and devotion to her classes, that her students started calling her "Mother" because she did mother as many as she could. They even inserted her name in the school fight song, which they kept singing many years after her retirement. She was a Senior Class sponsor, an advisor to the Student Government Association, and a director of the Senior Class Play for many years before schools had drama teachers, and was chosen as a STAR teacher one year by the school's top SAT score recipient.

Some members of the 1969 Senior Class, out of loving respect, decided to play a little trick. Mother managed those geography maps that scrolled up and down. She used them almost daily in her government discussions. This class had some pranksters who thought it would be funny to pull a joke on her. While she was on hall duty, a couple of boys from her 5th period class taped a *Playboy* magazine centerfold onto one of those world atlas maps and then rolled it back up into its cover. They planned to inquire about something in class that involved her having to pull down *that particular map* to answer the question they posed.

What they hadn't counted on was 3rd period getting involved. Someone in 3rd period innocently asked about a country that required my mother to pull down the atlas with the nude model plastered in the middle of it. Since she stood in front of the map while pulling it down, her body covered the diagram, and since no one expected the ruse, the students of that period didn't see it and she was able to tear the picture off without the rest of the class knowing the difference.

There was no way that the prank had spread around the school...yet. Fourth period passed with no drama. But then, 5th period showed up and those conniving guys, who just *knew* they were going to pull-one-over on their instructor, asked some question that was supposed to present the *Playboy* centerfold for everyone to see. Of course it actually backfired on them because without a doubt, they were the perpetrators that placed the nude model there in the first place.

Because it wasn't meant maliciously, I don't think those dudes that were caught got into too much trouble.

Oral Gratification

I seem to want to write about teeth a lot. Here's another...and another.

In 1967 I was a freshman in high school. I was taking French I along with just about every other 9th grader who was on the college prep track. I don't know why French was the most popular foreign language at the time rather than Spanish. High school classes in 1967 were designed to have seven periods lasting one hour and all classes lasted the entire year. In my French class we had 5 rows of students. Each row held at least 7 desks. You do the math.

Just about every freshman had something I wanted badly to fit in: glasses and braces. I didn't have the need to wear them but I wanted them so I could be like everyone else. Isn't that the way it always was? I had such straight teeth, dentists in my future told me, "You are *not* helping me pay for my dental practice." The only dental problems I had growing up were six fillings. Well, except for one big problem I inherited from birth: My mother's muscle frenum.

This was the space between your front teeth caused by the muscle behind them. Mine was on the upper front two teeth. It was so wide that I was able to stick my tongue through it sideways. I wanted to change that. The *Future-Valedictorian* of my 1971 Senior Class sat behind me. He was an excellent student and later, after graduating from Emory, became a dermatologist. He wore braces. The braces in the 1960s came with a string of tiny rubber bands which when placed on the upper and lower parts of the metal braces would pull teeth together, I think. I don't know. I never wore braces, remember? But I did want to get rid of that gap. I thought I looked like Alfred E. Newman, cover boy for *Mad Magazine*.

I asked this smart back-seat-neighbor, "Could I have a couple of your rubber bands?" I placed two rubber bands around my front four teeth during that one hour of French class, for two consecutive weeks, and *Voila*! My gap closed. And the best part was the space *never* opened up
again. I saved my parents hundreds of dollars. That was when I thought about going into dental school after college.

But that thought didn't last long after my next report card.

So I fixed my front tooth gap. I later had a bigger problem. When I told this incident to my high school students, I had to change it a little. Afterall, they were underage and it involved alcohol and I didn't want them to know such things, for their sake and mine.

While retelling the event, I referred to my long neck glass container that I was holding as a Coca-Cola bottle. But since you all are over the drinking age, *you know* what that amber bottle was in reality. So, from the beginning: I was in an establishment that served ice-cold foamy refreshments in tall bottles. While holding mine in my right hand near my mouth and while about to take a drink, someone shoved past me in that crowded establishment, hit my elbow causing the long neck to bump into a front tooth. Hurting, I rubbed my tongue over the spot and realized there was a crevice along the bottom edge.

When I returned home, I looked in my bathroom mirror and saw the open arc on my front tooth where there hadn't been one just the hour before. *OMGosh*! Now what? Can you guess what I did to correct that tooth chip? Since I am a do-it-yourselfer when it comes to dental improvements, I took my angel hair nail file and….*why not*? I was already anesthetized from the contents of that amber longneck glass bottle. I had to be careful not to take off too much so as to keep it pretty even with the twin tooth…or hit a nerve.

Don't let your dentist know about these dental tips. I am trying to help you out here, obviously, saving you big bucks for such little problems. I mean, I've been figuring out my own teeth dilemmas for years. At this moment, I've lost my tooth-grinding protector and am using a pacifier.

So, you're welcome, again.

Kissing Cuzins

I've been kissed by a President. Yup. You read that correctly.

After high school graduation and before attending college, I didn't have a summer job. I tried to enjoy those last free days before leaving home. That summer of 1971, I volunteered to help my county's chamber of commerce participate in the "Stay and See Georgia" campaign. The Georgia Department of Industry, Trade, and Tourism planned celebration activities at Lenox Square Mall, which in 1971 was an open-air mall with breezeways connecting the stores. They planned to bring together partners in Georgia's tourism industry to showcase Georgia's assets and spread a message of "Stay and See Georgia." Don't spend your travel dollars elsewhere. With 159 counties to choose among, they wanted travelers to stay and see what Georgia offered.

The campaign was one week long and several of us young girls manned the booth for our county. We wore our high school's matching cheerleading outfits so we would all look uniformed. The uniform top was a solid red vest with an Oxford cloth white Peter Pan collared shirt, which the length of the sleeves came to our elbow. We had on white knee socks with *still-in-my-closet* Bass Saddle Oxford shoes. The knee socks had a tassel at the fold at the top. The skirt was mighty short. It was only as long as your fingertips by your side. The uniform had a red and black pleated plaid skirt for our school colors.

Our county's only promoted treasure was a Roman Catholic Church. Our Lady of the Holy Spirit Monastery belonged to the worldwide Order of Cistercians of the Strict Observance, or more commonly known as Trappists. This tourist attraction had individuals of all faiths flock to the monastery. The day-to-day operations of the monastery are sustained through The Abbey Store, a stained glass manufacturing business, a bonsai garden plant and supply business, donations, a green cemetery, and onsite retreats. One can experience this serenity of restful recollection and spiritual renewal retreat on the 2,100 acres for a day, or as long as a week.

Later, in October 1990, a Conyers, Georgia homemaker by the name of Nancy Fowler claimed that the Virgin Mary appeared and instructed her to relay Mary's message to all citizens of the United States. The directive ranged from admonitions to prayers to warnings of war. The Virgin's supposed visits made Conyers one of the longest-lived Marian apparition sites in the nation. Roads going to Mrs. Fowler's home were clogged with pilgrims yearning to hear Mary's messages. Crowds as large as eighty thousand were not uncommon and Fowler had to broadcast her messages over loudspeakers. The overflow of people finally expanded from her yard to her next-door pasture. There they prayed in their native tongues – English, Spanish, Russian, and Chinese – filled bottles with water from the Blessed Well, and they opened a bookstore, where they even made and sold their own bumper stickers at the store that read, "*Eat, Drink, and See Mary!*" Not really. But the bumper stickers did exist.

Local government official became wary of the traffic, health, and safety problems and the Archdiocese of Atlanta became concerned that these unconfirmed visions might distract from the true faith. After 1998, pilgrimages to Conyers became less frequent.

But in 1971 we finished our week chatting with buyers at the mall and handing out brochures of information. The week-long promotional exhibit culminated when the Governor's Mansion held a reception for all participants. They feted us to munchies and punch for our week of hard work. We also stood in the receiving line to meet and thank our host and hostess, the Georgia governor and his wife.

Telling my aunt about our upcoming reception, she mentioned we were related – in the South we call it kin – to Jimmy Carter. While in line, I approached the couple. I shook Rosalyn's hand first and then when I was in front of the Governor, I said, "My aunt researched our family tree and found out we are cousins." I moved on to the next person to shake his hand. From my peripheral vision, I saw Jimmy Carter leaning in closer to me and then he planted a big kiss on my cheek and said, "I always kiss my cousins!"

Retelling this story years later in the late 1990s to a classroom full of high school students, I prefaced my story with "I have been kissed by a President."

Their response? "Who was it? Bill Clinton?"

Don't Cry for Me, Argentina

The President's agenda:
1) a promise to lead the people to victory in the presidential election
2) a promise to build a strong and just nation
3) a promise to eliminate poverty
4) a promise to dignify labor
5) a promise to reshape the economy

Trump? Or was it Obama?

Neither. It was Argentina's President, Juan Peron, who served from 1946 until 1955 when he was thrown out of his country.

My mother taught high school government in the 1950s. There was only one high school, therefore only one government teacher. But because government was a required credit to graduate, like it is today, everyone had to pass through her classroom.

One of her students had eventual influence on the national level in the political arena and you may have heard his name. Many more outstanding students passed through those halls after her retirement– an Oscar winner, Pulitzer Prize winner, professional athletes, and many other national success stories.

But this student sitting in her government classroom listened as she gave a government lesson about Juan Peron, the Argentinian general and politician who was elected three times as President of Argentina. Peron was overthrown in a military coup in 1955. She mentioned in this 1959 classroom, "Mark my words. Peron will be back." This gifted, young student must have taken her words to heart.

He graduated from high school and earned his B.B.A. in Economics from the University of Georgia in 1964. He became an assistant professor of Economics at Georgia State University. He later earned his Ph.D. in Economics in 1969 from the University of Virginia. As wonderful as this career seems, his star was still rising.

This young man's name was James C. Miller, III. In July 1985, President Ronald Reagan chose this "conservative economist who favors reducing the size of the federal government" as his administration's new budget director.

Before his rise in the Reagan administration and his movement up his brilliant career ladder, he must not have forgotten his high school roots and his government teacher. When Peron returned to power in 1973 (although briefly, as he served for nine months until his death in 1974 only to be succeeded by his third wife), Jimmy wrote a letter to my mother about this event, which she kept.

I am now retired myself and still wonder what kind of influence we teachers had on all our students after they became adults. My mother taught that Argentine lesson so many times that I am sure she didn't remember her own exact words when Jimmy Miller heard it. But he remembered.

His letter to her was brief. All it said was:

> *"Dear Teacher,*
> *You were right. Peron's back."*
>
> *Jimmy Miller*

I See Dead People

I tried to design all my classrooms in a cozy manner. I felt these teenagers learned best in a comfortable environment. If students and teachers spend more time in their day at their job/school than their own home, then I hoped my government-built-public-classroom felt like home away from home as much as possible.

I added big and little lamps to spread out the light rather than just having the overhead florescent lighting. I brought appropriate pictures and posters which I hung around the room regarding my literary subject. Along one wall there were long shelves and cabinets. I also added books, travel pictures, and family photos. Besides my family, I had photos of famous people that I admired.

While teaching in 2000, I wasn't quite over Princess Diana and John-John Kennedy's deaths, so, on a separate shelf, I placed their pictures in frames. These two photographs came from my home, where once they sat atop a drop leaf table in my den along with various family and friends' pictures. For fun, I put their pictures mixed in with my family ones to fool guests and see if they recognized these well-known celebrities among my household portraits. Besides John-John and Lady Di, *Hubby* had taken a close-up picture of Jack Nicklaus when he was a spectator at Pebble Beach Golf Club. Once a gal visited my house and perused my dozens of pictures on the table when her eyes stopped and stared at JFK, Jr. She said, "This person sure does look familiar."

Uh, yeah.

So, with Princess Di and John Kennedy, Jr's impressions standing out on my shelves, a student came up one day and asked me while pointing to those two, "Mrs. St. John, why do you have *those* pictures in your room?"

I explained how I adored them before they died and just wanted to have their photographs around because they meant so much to me at one time and that they died much too soon.

He then said, "Well don't go putting *my* picture on your shelf because all you've got up there are *dead people*."

Same Song...

In 2010, I went to the 10-year reunion for the Class of 2000. It was great seeing all those guys. Some I had not seen in a decade. These students had many accomplishments during those ten years. Some were married! Some were extremely successful! Some had children! Where had the decade gone?

At the reunion, one former student came up to me and told me, "*To this day*, I still quote you." Well, that was flattering but I thought, "Uh, oh. What was so noteworthy that I am quoted continually?" So, I asked.

He said, "It was the quote you always told us: 'I'm sorry. I didn't mean to be talking while you were interrupting.'"

Oh. Great line. I used it a lot when I was trying to get my students' attention. Administrators told us not to use sarcasm in the classroom but that one was just too good to pass up. I don't remember where I stole that quote from because I'm sure I didn't make it up. The thing about that line was that it was not the first time I had used it. I taught in every decade from the 1970s until 2009. Not every year of every decade, just every decade. That made 4 decades. If I had stayed one year longer (2010), I could have said, "I am only 56 years old and yet I have taught in five decades." Think about it.

I used that line, in every decade that I taught...the 1970s, the 1980s, the 1990s, and the 2000s, however, the reactions were different as the decades passed. In the late 1970s – 1980s, when my students spoke off-topic too much and started conversations of their own about anything else but the subject, I'd say that line and their response? "Oh, Mrs. St. John. We are *sooooooo* sorry." And they stopped talking at that very moment.

The 1990s reaction: "Oh, Mrs. St. John. We're sorry." But it took them a bit to calm down to how I expected to conduct themselves.

The 2000s reaction: "Oh." And they kept on talking.

I might be exaggerating – a little – and not all students were like that, but this description is pretty close. Now I know why our parents would say in front of us while were growing up in the 1960s and 1970s, "What is happening to this new generation? No respect for authority." I guess every older generation wonders what is happening to the manners of the generation on deck.

It Ain't Gonna Get Moi Très Loin.

Bonjour!
Pourquoi ai-je prendre des cours de français au secondaire ? Ce qu'il a été bon pour moi ? Bien sûr, je peux aller dans un restaurant français et dire, "Garcon !" quand je veux commander un verre d'eau, mais la lecture du menu ? It ain't gonna get moi très loin.

Translation: Why did I take French in high school? What good has it been to me? Sure, I can go into a French restaurant and say, "Garçon!" when I want to order a glass of water, but reading the menu? It isn't gonna get me very far.

See? After taking French I and II in high school and a year in college, this is what it amounts to. Oh, I've even been to Paris... twice. It's a beautiful romance language but they weren't very impressed when I spoke the little French I did remember which was: "French Fries", "French Dressing", and "French Kissing". And I am also crazy about Country French Décor. Maybe all this appreciation for all things French comes from my DNA. I am a descendent of French Huguenots on my maternal grandfather's side.

Sometimes I become giddy and just break out into a French accent for the fun of it. And although in my head it sounds like the native tongue, I know it comes out just like Pepe Le Pew, the fictional cartoon character from the Warner Brother's *Looney Tunes and Merri Melodies* (and with my heritage you'd think I'd perfected it). First introduced in 1945, Le Pew is depicted as a French striped skunk constantly in search of love. But his offensive skunk odor and aggressiveness in the pursuit of romance causes other characters to flee from him in fear while he hops after them in leisurely pursuit.

Pepe Le Pew's storylines typically involve his quest of a female black cat, Penelope Pussycat, whom he mistakes for a skunk ("la belle femme skunk fatale"). This black cat squeezed under a newly painted fence and is unaware that wet white paint caused a white stripe down her back. Of course this attracts Le Pew but every time he tries to embrace her she frantically races to get away from him because of his putrid odor. He never loses confidence no matter how many times he is rebuffed. These escapades are always set in exotic locales in France associated in popular culture with romance, such as the Champs-Elysees or the Eiffel Tower.

"And zee? Ah con speek jus liake hem." (Think of a French accent when you read that.)

Once when putting my best French forward, I made a rather funny faux pas. In 1976, I had been working one summer at the Omni International Hotel in Atlanta. I was answering the phone for the catering department. The hotel's main restaurant prepared French cuisine. Hors D'oeuveres were délicieux. Des salades were magnifique. Entrees were attrait. Desserts were exquisite.

When the phone rang, I answered and a woman on the other end spoke, "Hello. Could you please read the list of the entrée choices in the main restaurant tonight?"

When I started reading from the poisson section a delicious favorite stood out. The recipe's name, according to French lore, is referenced to a miller of wheat whose wife cooked everything coated with flour. The original French style of cooking this fish, then, was seasoned and floured, sautéed in butter, and finally topped with the brown butter from the pan. It was listed on the menu as Trout Meunière, which with my haste and poor French skills I delivered this enticing dish as *trout manure*.

A Day in the Life of a Teacher

High School Version

I was called to take a long-term substitute job for a high school teacher out on maternity leave. I had retired but I had known the teacher for many years because we worked in the same department. The school knew I was proficient with the subject matter, as I had taught this grade level before she was hired.

I had been gone long enough that these students did not know me. And I was older. Were these students contemplating how to pull the wool over my eyes because I didn't know their names, their reputations, or their parents? I think not. I was one step ahead. I brought out my cassette recorder, blank tape, and set up shop to record their antics of the day.

After class, one student must have warmed up to me and he started a conversation about all the great vacations he and his family had taken. They were able to afford them because every weeknight at 6:59 on the Atlanta channel WSB-TV, they watched the Georgia Lottery announcements. They never played the lottery. Instead of buying tickets, they wrote their winning numbers down ahead of time, brought their money, and waited for the pronouncement of the numbers by the host. Because they never won, they pooled all their family money into a vacation pot and that was how they afforded those great vacations.

I thought that was clever.

Hearing about the cassette recorder that I was using for class allowed the rest of the day to go without incident and when I arrived home that night I realized that I wasn't just the sub for day but for the next six weeks. I was old and tired and since I was the "real" teacher in charge, I had to do "real" teacher things, like grade the essays that were left on the "real" teacher's desk before her emergency maternity leave.

I took them home, and that night before dinner, poured a humongous glass of wine and started reading and correcting the students' work. You know how that worked out, right? Yep, the best-written papers that received the best grades were at the bottom of the heap.

College

Broadway Joe

Growing up in my small town, there was a wonderful gentleman who owned a five-and-dime variety story. The high school seniors leaving for college for the first time were the recipients of his generosity. There was only one high school at the time, so it wasn't a hardship for him to be so generous. He pulled together a collection of items from his store, packaged them, and mailed them to the college freshmen a few weeks after the university school year started. It made us feel at home in case we were homesick.

He sent a package to me in the fall of 1971. The package contained all kinds of goodies from his store: fireballs, wax bottles with colored sugar water in them, Bit O'Honey candy, gum, pencils, erasers, spiral notebooks, those big 'ole red wax lips, and such…just what you'd find in a five and dime emporium. Mine came within the first month of school. The box was wrapped in brown paper with string tied around it. Since I did not know about this hometown gentleman's generosity for incoming freshmen and only found out later he had been providing these treats for many years, I was confused about this package's arrival. The return address said, "Joe Willie Namath. Shapula, Mississippi."

I brought the package to my dorm from the college's central mailroom. I began opening it in the community living room on my hall. In 1971 we lived in all-female dormitories that had two girls to a room, a large community bathroom/showers per floor for all the girls, and a community living room for the entire hall. The living room had one TV and you had better get used to sharing it. There was only one wall phone for all the girls living on a floor and I think there might have been 40 girls to a floor. Get used to sharing that phone, also.

My roommate and I knew each other in high school. We had the most fun decorating our room with coordinating bedspreads and pillows. She loved daisies and our room was yellow and white. It was very bright. We had bulletin boards along the side of our single beds, which we could pull out for sleeping, but when not used as a bed, could be pushed back against the wall to be used as a sofa. One side of the bed was used for storage and it was padded and could be opened up from bottom to top like an airplane overhead bin to store your luggage. While opening the package that arrived that day, my neighbor from next door came down to see what was happening. Packages without the recipient's knowledge were like little surprise parties.

She asked who sent it. I told her what the return address said and then…I had an idea. I decided to prank her for as long as she'd let me.

I lied, "I met Joe Namath last year in New York City, but I never expected this!"

She was totally astonished. I didn't know it at the time but later found out that she and her dad were *big* University of Alabama fans and she knew who Joe Namath was. She exclaimed loudly, "You *know* Joe Namath? How did you meet him?"

This was going to be fun.

"Well, my dad, as a coach (true) was asked to attend this national high school coach's conference in New York (not true) and mother and I tagged along (not true). The guest speaker was Joe Namath. After his speech, I went up to him, like dozens of others, and told him how much I enjoyed his speech. We started talking after people left. We wrote a few times, but I never thought I'd receive a gift from him."

I owned her.

To keep up the ruse throughout the year, whenever Broadway Joe was on a TV commercial for Beautymist Pantyhose, or Noxema's "take it off" shaving cream, I threw out my ammunition and made comments like, "Joe likes the color blue," or "Did I ever mention Joe loves pepperoni pizza?" or anything else that might have come up for me to build my deception.

Near the end of the school year, surprisingly, I received another package from the Variety-Store-Owner. My dormitory neighbor saw I had another parcel and jealously asked, "Who is it from? *Joe Namath*?"

Well, I knew I was going to have to confess before we left for summer break. I couldn't let her go home for the summer with my lie.

"I can't believe it!" she yelped. "When I went home to Savannah to visit, I told everyone I know that I have a friend who knows Joe Namath!"

Well, it should end there. But this practical joke made it back to my hometown before I did and there was story in the local newspaper about the shenanigan. Then the *Atlanta Constitution* (now the *Atlanta Journal Constitution*) picked up the story through the wire service and introduced it on their editorial page.

Luckily for me, my friend's family didn't take the *AJC* in Savannah.

Drawing from Experience

In high school, I was never a great student. My poor mother. She was a brainiac and I knew I totally embarrassed her among her peers. Don't get me wrong: I *loved* high school but only the pageantry of it. I joined every club possible my senior year. I wanted to have my picture in the yearbook often. I even practiced signing my signature so it would look pretty on the pages. Here I was "playing high school" when all she wanted was for me to be interested in my studies. I was in so many clubs and activities that in my senior year annual my pictures were on one-third of the pages. And see how awful it is to even remember that? That's how important school was to me then. I was a social butterfly.

So when it was time for college – and yes, I did get in one – I thought about majoring in music. I had taken piano lessons for nine years. I also was a soloist for church, in my school's trio, school chorus, and I had already been invited to sing for a few weddings while still in high school. But I needed advice. Who would you turn to? The school counselors, of course.

However, counselors before 1971 never spoke with anyone I knew to give advice about what classes to take to improve your chances of getting into college…much less a *great* college. I think there were two counselors in my school. Whenever I saw one or the other, they were heading to lunch or their office and then they closed their doors. They handled "scheduling." That's all I ever heard about them. I never even knew who my assigned counselor was and I never heard anyone say they had met with one to discuss their future.

Walking in the hall one day, I thought I saw something.

"Is that my counselor?" I asked another student.

"Heck, if I know," was the answer. "Whoever it is, I saw her at lunch and now she is heading back to her office to close the door."

Nine months later I finally got a good look at her because she had her picture taken for the yearbook. (Just *one* picture – I counted and I had her beat.) That's the only way I knew who she was: underneath her picture I saw her name the word – counselor.

So when I left for college I had concluded I should major in music with piano as my instrument. Then I changed my mind and decided I'd still major in music but my instrument should be voice. Nah. I replaced that idea with Art. That was it! *Art.*

I registered for the mandatory core and art classes. I enjoyed my art classes, I really did. I had taken art in high school and I think that I had 3 pictures on the art club page. I liked the teacher. I liked the fellow students. I liked drawing, although it was isolating and not a very social major. Spring quarter rolled around and the beauty of the season was teeming with all the white dogwoods blooming, the yellow and white daffodils popping up, the soft green grass between our toes, and the pink azaleas in bloom at this southern Georgia college. With all this natural beauty, our professor asked us to take inspiration from our art lab windows, since we had tons of them, to see the exquisiteness of Spring and draw however we felt motivated.

Our core classes were offered the first part of the day and art lab classes were offered at the end of the day. So our vision was the late afternoon warm sun before its end. And since it was April, what I saw resulted in a major change for me (double entendre!) I saw students sitting in lounge chairs or lying on beach towels on the campus grounds, applying suntan lotion, listening to music, and drinking beer.

I was inspired all right. It was then I knew I had to get my priorities in order. I saw what I was missing out of college. I changed my major a fourth time at the end of the quarter.

What do 18-year old students know anyway?

What You See Is What You Get

Summer school at Georgia Tech.

There was not a lot of entertainment offered as in the regular school year: football, baseball, frat parties, independent socials, and other activities that involved large crowds. It was rather a slow evening when two of my teacher friends were on campus attending a concert at the Alexander Memorial Coliseum in the 1980s. These gals were married with small children but decided on a night out in Atlanta. The duo chose to go to a concert that their husbands were not interested in attending so, they made it an girls-only event. The hubbies kept the children while their wives high-tailed it to "Hot'lanta" for the evening.

Not knowing their way around the Georgia Tech campus very well, they did not find a parking space close to the coliseum and they had to park several blocks away. They were pushing forty and were still very attractive women. Summer meant they dressed in short shorts, sleeveless shirts, and jeweled sandals. They had big hair and dark tans like most females in the 1980s. Around dusk, the gals walked from their car through fraternity row – usually an inebriated and hormonal part of the campus. As they approached one particular fraternity house, my teacher friends saw several young men in front of the house on the sidewalk.

As the sunlight dimmed on the tree-lined path, they saw these boys starting to nudge each other, talking lively and loudly, and were posturing themselves to show off in front of these gals. These girls were looking good…unlike the saying, "The more you drink, the better I look." I mean, they were really attractive and they could tell by the approaching boys' behavior that these dudes thought so, too…until…both parties met.

These goofy guys who had sex on the brain and had been whooping it up and hollering to attract these women from more than thirty yards away in diminished sunlight, now realized what they were seeing. And my friends heard one yell to another, "Oh, they are just old women."

Hook, Line, and Sinker

After I married, the pond on our thirty-acre property was a real lifesaver when it came to clean entertainment for our boys. That lake had all kinds of fish in it – bass, bream, catfish, and crappie. When I lived there with my parents before I married, my dad had a little cocktail-party-hobby every other evening. He bought a bag of fish food from the feed and seed store, took several full cups of the dry fish food along with his stiff vodka on the rocks for himself, and walked down the lake road around five o'clock in the afternoon on the alternating evenings with both pleasures in hand – one for him and one for the fish.

He stood on the banks of the three-acre pond and watched all the activity. The fish were used to this routine and they kicked up their tails at the top of the water while waiting for their treat. Dad threw out the fish food and they gobbled it right up. If you wanted to catch fish, now was the time, but where was the sport in that? We didn't do that. At this point they were almost pets. Because I went with him many times, he and I sat down on the camp stools at water's edge and enjoyed the moment and later the sunset.

I learned to fish from my dad. I enjoyed it immensely. When I attended college, I took a physical education course called Bait Casting 101. What a shoo-in I'd be. And I was going to meet some guys! How many girls were really going to take a course like that? But the irony was the course wasn't offered in the spring at a lake on the campus grounds. It was offered in the winter in the basketball gymnasium and taught by the university basketball coach.

He set up half-court with a bullseye that was used in the physical education archery classes. Every ten yards from center there would be another bullseye. And another. And another. There were four. Students had to cast their fishing pole (with a drop weight and not a lure) and hit the yellow center circle for an "A". The next color was red for a "B", then the blue circle was a "C", and finally if you hit black all the time you made a "D". There was a white circle but I don't remember anyone making an "F". As a matter of fact, there were only eight students in that class. Seven males. One female. I liked my odds.

The fishing rod that I kept after my P.E. class was a 7-foot medium action Ugly Stick with a ten-pound test line on a Zebco pushbutton reel. That lucky pole and my wrist action brought home a "B", which I think was the best grade in the class beating out all those boys who thought a girl couldn't pull off the highest grade.

I Heard It Through the Grapevine

This story was passed around so much when I was in college. I was told by a friend whose cousin, who also had a friend whose other friend knew the guy who 'originally' told this anecdote and who said he was told by his cousin who knew the guy first hand. Whew. That means it had to be true, right?

Sometimes couples worry about who might pull a prank on them before, during, or after the wedding and reception. A friend of mine knew a groom who knelt down in prayer with his bride during the ceremony at the front of the church when some of the congregation started snickering. Someone had grabbed his shoes ahead of the ceremony so when he stooped down on his knees in prayer, his shoes' soles faced out to the congregation and he had no idea that with the help of a black magic marker, the underbelly of his shoes read, "*Help Me!*" Those sitting in the church pews closest to the couple read 'his plea' and giggled.

When my cousin married, his buddies made a sign for his car that read, "Her Day. His Night." That was a good one. The groom in this story had every reason to be nervous. While still in college, he was the first of his pledge class in his fraternity to get married. All those fraternity brothers were really close and tended to try to one-up each other over their college years at the University of Georgia. The pranks were harmless unlike what you might think, or have heard in recent years, but they still were pranks and came about at the most vulnerable moments. He himself had played some extremely clever and wicked tricks on others and he knew he was due his turn and what better place to play a gag on him to 'get even' than his own pre or post-wedding nuptials?

He looked over his back at every turn. Once, my *Atlanta-Partner-In-Crime* worried that several of her friends were going to embarrass her during her rehearsal dinner. There was a great song by Marilyn McCoo that we kept singing every time that she was around entitled, "Wedding Bell Blues*"* where my *Atlanta-Partner-In-Crime* would sing, "Won't you marry me, Bill?" Her Bill did marry her and she knew we were going to do something silly like start singing it when we stood up to give a toast at her rehearsal dinner in this gorgeous banquet room at a fancy Atlanta country club. She didn't mind her future-husband seeing us mis-behave that way; it was her future-mother-in-law she was worried about. She wanted to start her marriage with a mature image.

But the groom in this story stayed afraid of retaliation for weeks on end. The bachelor party was even calm for his crew. He sweated bullets through his rehearsal dinner but nothing came of it. He thought the worst was yet to come – the wedding. What would they do to hijack the show? The jittery soon-to-be-husband stayed in a state of high-anxiety. That, too, passed without a hitch.

"Ok." this college senior thought, "It *has* to be the reception. They are going to zing me there." He stayed uptight watching and waiting and again, nothing out of the ordinary. He had been on edge for his bride, her parents and their friends, his parents and their friends, and himself. But the entire ceremony and celebration came and went with the utmost decorum of a wedding at that cost. He dodged a bullet.

Now, he was scot-free! No more anxiety. He knew *no one* had any idea where he and his bride were going on their honeymoon. He kept all the planning close to his vest. He wasn't about to give those fraternity brothers any ammunition to thwart the last detail. So, off they went. They flew to Bora Bora, French Polynesia, in the South Pacific. They were out of the country and away from any distress. He relaxed on the flight and calmly checked into their hut on a palm-shaded Polynesian beachfront and crystalline lagoon. These honeymoon bungalows were built atop a lagoon and were private and breathtaking. They were in heaven on earth.

Before going to dinner for the first time as man and wife, even though extremely tired from the long flight, this couple decided to consummate their marriage. Alone, quiet, and full of love, they enjoyed their moments of privacy until…they had discovered the marital setting had been invaded after all by one of his college frat brothers who had traveled all that way to demonstrate the *Gotcha* of all *Gotchas*! This dude previously had hidden under the marital bed and was quiet as a mouse until the marital celebrations were over and then slithered out to surprise the couple at the most inappropriate moment.

I don't think there are many stories that can top that.

Miss Right?
or Miss Right Now?

Hubby and I recently returned from a destination wedding of a college buddy's son. While out of state, many of the *baby-boomers* enjoyed a brunch the morning after the ceremony and started discussing our own memories of how we met our spouses. We "old-timers" had a fun time swapping stories from decades before.

My husband's fraternity brother, the *Groom's Dad*, told his story but then he went right into one that was a real hoot. A college friend of his was visiting Atlanta and hooting and hollering it up in a bar on Peachtree Street. The friend was with some other carousing dudes. They were having such a good time, in fact, that one of the guys in the group fell off a bar stool and broke his leg. Luckily for them, Piedmont Hospital was just down Peachtree Street and the party boys gathered up this broken friend, placed him in their car, and headed for the hospital's emergency room.

While there, they sobered up, rose to the occasion, and answered all the questions about the accident posed by the doctors on call. They were mature, serious, and forthcoming about the details of the incident. But when the young man with the broken bones was admitted to the back room for further examination, they were left waiting around in the hospital emergency room lobby with nothing to do until there was further news about their friend. Now these young bucks had responsibly done their duty and all that was left for them was to wait it out and bring their friend home. So, what would a young man after a night of drinking do to kill time?

They started flirting with the nurses.

Groom's Dad's friend was especially enamored with one student nurse. He was able to grab a few minutes of her time and trying to make an impression, he chatted about this and that with her when he could in between her shift. He thought he made a good first impression but knew he couldn't make a real move on her because she was working.

So, the next day, he called the hospital, was put through to the Emergency Room, asked someone who answered the phone to help him find this adorable student nurse he had met the night before and who he tried to impress. He gave the caller her description in detail (or maybe just what he remembered after a night of libations?). The medical assistant on the phone said, "Oh, *Nurse Betty*? Yes, she was here working last night."

He then asked to speak to *Nurse Betty*. She eventually was able to answer the phone and speak to *Groom's Dad's* friend. He flirted some more with his witty words and asked her if she remembered 'this' which they talked about and 'that' he was sure she'd recall, but she didn't. She explained that it was a very busy night in the emergency room in the hospital the evening before and she just didn't recollect some of the things he was saying.

He wanted to meet her and he mentioned to meet up for a drink at Harrison's, a bar just down the street from the hospital and ironically where the accident occurred. He told her he would be wearing an orange Auburn sweater and a few other descriptions so that when she arrived, she could find him easily.

The nurse walked in, saw this young man by his depiction, sat down at his table, and the first words out of the college boy's mouth were, "You're the wrong one."

He and "the wrong one" have been married over forty years.

Who Could It Be Now?

Take your pick: a fabrication, a myth, or an urban legend. Whatever it is, this story was told to me as truth. And when it came to extremely smart, bored, mischievous students' hi-jinx in the 1960s at the University of Georgia, I believed it.

UGA is the flagship school for the state of Georgia. It is big. *Big*! Today's enrollment is over 36,000 students. You had better have some self-control to attend there. It could chew you up and spit you out if you weren't disciplined enough. I'd always known that the really, really, smart genius-type of students had their own kind of pranks. Today they might hack into computers, but in the 1960s they were pulling different escapades. Still shocking but in this instance not harmful to others.

A group of boys created a phantom student, a nonreal, yet class attending, test-taking undergraduate. Now I can't tell you specifics, but this made up pupil enrolled, was accepted, paid tuition, and graduated in 4 years. I don't know *who* these devil-may-care creators were, I don't know how many were involved to pull this prank off, but I heard that at the end of four years, this student, whose name I forgot but very similar sounding to Alfred E. Neuman from *MAD Magazine*, was simply a figment of their imagination.

They could get away with it at the time because enrollment and test taking were all done with a #2 pencil and scan sheets. If one enrolled in a general education core class or a popular major where the classes met in large auditoriums, the professors at the time were not able to identify students or track them as easily. This ruse went on for four years. The guys pooled their money and paid for this hallucination's entire education. They continued their hi-jinx for four years! Now that's dedication.

The tricksters may have duplicated their efforts if they themselves were in a certain major, let's say a general business major, and pull this off. Take two tests at one time with a student number they made up from the beginning. It was possible.

And when graduation came, a diploma was waiting for this mirage. His name was called and called and no such person responded on stage to receive it. Those who initiated this spoof had a grand time knowing they pulled it off.

You don't have to believe it if you don't want to.

Do You Know Who I Am?

Another rumor surfaced about a young, confident, and cocky student. Now I have to admit I have recently seen this scenario on a *YouTube* video. But there was no *YouTube* in the 1970s when I first heard this account. They must have reenacted it since I first knew of this story.

At the time of enrollment to the University of Alabama in the early 1970s, a well-known student had been a big fish in a big pond at his Mountain Brook, Alabama high school. He didn't feel intimidated by attending Alabama as a freshman because he had an older brother who preceded him there and showed him the ropes. Mountain Brook is a suburb of Birmingham and one of the state's most affluent places to live. Because his older brother had already blazed the trail for him, the younger brother's reputation was heralded even though he had just arrived on campus.

His brother had already laid the necessary groundwork for him, ran interference, and just smoothed the way for his little brother. Plus, a lot of his high school friends were also attending the university. The younger brother got into the "right" fraternity, as a freshman became a "big brother" to one of the top sororities, and because of his name recognition from Mountain Brook, he just sailed through that first year. He was smart but so far hadn't applied himself. He partied and played as though his college education was secondary. And to him it was. If he kept this up, his popularity might even lead him to be Student Council President. Heck, a future senator. Let's not think small – *President*!

But at the moment, he was lazy and didn't apply himself. He was coasting through his classes. This well-known young man was presumptuous, felt entitled, and let's face it: he was. He was getting away with this behavior and was going to ride this wave as long as he could. Taking a mandatory freshman course, you might find yourself with hundreds of other newbies checking off a required class for graduation. This overconfident undergraduate saw himself in an auditorium full of students, where 300 or so sat to receive information from an obligatory course he was taking and sometimes with a professor who wished he didn't have to teach to the masses.

He felt he could skip many of these classes, study the subject matter on his own, and still pass the course – instructor or no instructor. There weren't many with this nerve. He felt he was one-in-a-million. In reality, he was in a sea of students who were only numbers on the professor's roll. They never added their names to tests. They just wrote a number assigned to them. The instructors were dealing with quantity in this large venue. They never knew, on a personal level, which students were in their classes. And when grading, they just distributed a grade to a student number.

The day before the final exam, this dude did shows up, however late, for the auditorium's class. It peeved the instructor that this pupil walked in *late* after the slamming of the heavy hall doors disrupted the professor's lecture and with the student climbing over several others in the row took a non-assigned seat. The instructor made a point at the end of the class to tell the students that the next day their final exam would take the entire period of class and asked that *no one* be late, as they could not finish the exam by the end of class if they were tardy. And you know to whom this statement was directed.

The next day, the undergrad again made a late appearance, with the same commotion, and took a seat where there was a copy of the test already laid out. It perturbed the teacher, but he let it go as the students were now involved in the quiet test taking and by making a big deal about it would disrupt those who had already started the exam.

When time was about over, students filed down the aisle of the auditorium and laid their test sheets on the professor's table at the front of the assembly hall. More students brought their tests down as the deadline approached. The professor announced to the remaining few that "Time is up in five minutes" as a warning that the class would be over soon and to start wrapping up any final answers.

They acted on his request, all except the late student. Not only did he not return his paper to the professor on time, he continued to write for a few more minutes. When he finally brought his paper to the instructor's table, the faculty member said to him, "I told all the students yesterday to be on time as the test would take up the entire class period. I wasn't going to allow you to have extra time, but I did, and I shouldn't have. I am going to deduct from your grade."

Without missing a beat and with hundreds of unnamed students on the professor's class list on his side, the arrogant young man still holding his test in his hand asked, "Do you know who I am? Do you know who my father is?"

The instructor looked in disbelief at the brash young man and commented, "I do not and I don't care who your father is."

With that, the student who was just one of many pupils to the teacher, picked up about half of the other numbered completed exams from the pile, placed his somewhere in the stack, restored the mound of papers to the condition he found it, and turned around and walked out of the auditorium.

You Can't Go Home Again

Author Thomas Wolfe wrote and published his books from the 1920s to the 1940s reflecting on American culture and mores of that period including the stock market crash, the illusion of prosperity, and the passing of time, which he called "unfair" because it prevents one from ever being able to return "home again."

One of his novels, *You Can't Go Home Again*, reinforces his main character's disillusionment. "You can't go back home to your family, back home to your childhood…back home to a young man's dreams of glory and of fame…back home to places in the country, back home to the old forms and systems of things which once seemed everlasting but which are changing all the time – back home to the escapes of Time and Memory."

One of my longest and dearest girlfriends, Swoozie, became a sorority's House-mother after retiring from her career. It is perfect for her. While at the University of Georgia, she was president of her sorority, Alpha Omega Pi. So this job is just an extension of that, sorta. She is partly paid by having her own rent-free apartment and free-meal plan in the house.

Around the Christmas holidays before the semester ended, I recently visited her place and it is precious! She gives a new definition to the term, house-mother. Some house-mothers of yester-year were frumpy and lacked imagination or personality, and were rather domineering. Maybe they had to be for the times…after all, it *was* the 70s. But Swoozie can not only make the hard decisions concerning house management (she was a business major at UGA herself), she also runs the house with heart. My friend was hiding her own version of elf-on-a-shelf for the girls, sitting and eating beside with them at meals, and welcoming any young lady who might be in need of a hug or counseling without sounding like a disciplinarian or helicopter house-mother.

She transitioned easily into the role.

But what an awakening for me! Of course I didn't expect it to be the way it was when I attended college. And although I was nostalgic at being in a sorority house again, fondly looking at their framed compositions of pictures of the sisters from each year, and the freedom we had of coming and going without having to be held accountable by our parents, it was just, well, different.

The home's large living area(s) was decorated in the sorority colors with stylish and upscale furniture. Ours was very much on a small scale because we only had around forty sisters. The 2019 class had *hundreds*. And while I was there, these girls were studying...*studying really hard* in majors like molecular chemistry, Russian literature, bi-lingual studies, and not just a business degree, they were done with that; they were stepping up to the next level and going for graduate program degrees. Quite an impressive accomplishment!

Scarce are the careers of my youth - teachers, nurses, journalism, and one of the most coveted – that M.R.S. degree. (Not that there aren't teachers, nurses, journalism, and M.R.S. degrees being awarded and received with pride.) There are more choices.

I always told my students to prepare themselves for their future by networking. Sure, make good-enough grades, but remember to socialize, too. More Chief Executive Officers made C's in college. How did they become successful? They were well rounded. First, they joined fraternities, other clubs on campus, or found their niche in theater, music, band, or athletics. They buddied-up with all kinds of people because those people, too, were networking. After college, it's the "Who You Know" (and maybe the Who-You-Know-And-Their-Daddies, too) syndrome. At that time, they weren't looking at your college transcripts. At the time it was more about knowing your character, and who better to know you and give glowing introduction for that first job but those friends from college and their parents.

One should prepare oneself academically, but connecting with people is *just* as important. Every one of my first starts in my different careers – teaching, journalism, real estate -were through the connections of someone I knew, or my parents knew, or a college/sorority friend helped me with. And in UGA's sorority houses they are coming in and out of that front door at all times for meetings, philanthropy planning, and other community services. There is your instant networking right there.

Nostalgia is a fond memory. It arises out of an absent person's inability to perceive changes that take place over time. The memories are static and permanent and attempting to relive those youthful remembrances is doomed to failure. You can't go home again, but you can learn time-honored lessons of self-improvement for future successes.

And my house-mother-friend? She got her job by knowing other house-mothers and by being a sorority girl herself.

The Breakfast of Champions

My father played baseball for Oglethorpe University. He was the first person in his county to ever receive a collegiate athletic scholarship. He was a 6'2" 180-pound southpaw (left-handed pitcher). The year was 1934 and in the spring of that year he was just 19 years old. In 1936, he was issued an invitation to the Summer Olympics held in Berlin, Germany. Baseball was being considered for inclusion in future Olympic competitions as a sport. First it had to be introduced to the Olympic Committee in an exhibition. And the Olympic Committee members, who were from around the world, were in one place that summer – Berlin. All one has to say today is "1936 Summer Olympics" to know those special stories surrounding Jesse Owens and Adolf Hitler.

My father had no sponsor to help offset the cost of playing in Germany that summer. He was an amateur. All the boys who were invited to perform were. They would all leave their homes that summer and just play ball in front of the committee so that they *might* decide the future of baseball in Olympic competition. He had to raise one hundred dollars to fund his trip and he said he couldn't raise ten dollars at the time. His scholarship to Oglethorpe gave him free tuition, room, and board in recognition for the sports he played, which were not only baseball but also basketball. That meant his education was paid for winter quarter (basketball) and spring quarter (baseball).

Since he did not play football, those classes came out of pocket. He worked every summer to make enough money to pay for the fall classes and his spending money. My students were always dumbfounded that he didn't play that exhibition game at the 1936 Olympics because my daddy loved baseball, of course. But he valued education above all. And his sport, which later offered him a pro contract with the Chicago Cubs, didn't come with such things as a *NIKE* endorsement or being on the cover of a *WHEATIES* cereal box. It wasn't about the big bucks at that time.

So the summer before the fall quarter, the one where he would have been in Berlin playing ball but missing the opportunity to earn money for his education, seems almost surreal today. Wouldn't somebody help a kid out? It was 1936. The stock market crash of 1929 happened just seven years earlier and America was still rebounding. People didn't have a lot of extra money to give away. He had to earn it himself. And he earned it for school – not a trip to Germany for the summer and missing the only time to raise money for his education.

The team he was chosen to play on at the exhibition game (Let's say *Team A*) won the contest between the two assigned teams and the player that took his spot was from Auburn. Baseball became an official Olympic sport at the 1992 Summer Olympics. It was last played in 2008.

He eventually received his degree from Oglethorpe, contracted and played ball for the Cubs, married, and had a family.

Priorities.

Southern Shenanigans

Someone Left the Gate Open

After the widespread effort to rig the college admissions process for children whose parents were willing to pay bribes, here is lighthearted take on the fascinating world of the Gatekeepers: those in charge of accepting or rejecting students who, in a distinctly American rite of passage, apply for colleges all across the United States.

Dear University of Southern California Admissions,

I will be graduating in May from Bunkum Senior High in Maine. I had not planned to attend college but now that I see there are two openings on your crew team, I informed my parents last night I wanted to apply.

They both said, "Rowing? That's not a mainstream (pun intended) sport."

"True," I answered, "but the YouTube videos I watched mentioned it was a great sport that offers a chance to start at an older age. I mean, no one has been rowing since childhood. I was thinking maybe that's how a Hollywood celebrity was able to get her children on a crew athletic scholarship. They never rowed before. It also provides overall body conditioning and I can get in great shape since you always say I spend too much time in front of my computer and not enough time outside. I can make new friends since you don't like the ones I hang with anyway. You think I stay so isolated in my room so this is an opportunity to learn teamwork, too."

Mother continued, "Honey, remember all those times when you and your dad went deep sea fishing in Destin when you were a little boy? You had to take Dramamine to keep from getting seasick on the boat."

I reminded them, "I grew out of that."

They reiterated, "That's because you stopped going."

"Well," I interjected, "What's your point?"

They pointed out, "That's just one reason. Another is you don't know how to swim!"

I commented, "That used to be true. But I am mature now and would like to learn. I never liked to get wet and I don't have to being a crew member. I mean, sure, they'll be splashing oars and wet boats, but since I'll be wearing a spandex, not cotton, unisuit, that shouldn't be a problem. And when I finally have some chiseled muscles from the year-round practices and the girls see me in that spandex, watch out USC!"

My father asked, "We don't want to discourage you from finally wanting to go to college, but can't you pick another direction and another school?"

"Rowing is the oldest intercollegiate sport in the United States, dating back to 1852. Who doesn't want to feel like a Viking on the open sea?"

And with that, they gave up. But not me.

I hope you will see my determination to row at your fine university. I plan to study pre-law because as you can see, I made some pretty good arguments with my parents.

Sincerely,

Lawrence Nightengail

P.S. Do you have to see my grades or can my parents just pay for admission since there is a precedent set?

P.S.S. I am also applying to UCLA, Wake Forest, and other *Operation Varsity Blues* universities. But since you are my first choice, I hope to hear from you soon.

College Admissions Essay to Harvard
by
Sunny Day

Dear Harvard University Admissions,

It has long been a dream of mine to attend Harvard. I will be great asset to your college community because every movie I see about Harvard, no one is smiling. Everyone is so serious. Is it the weather? Is it the stress? Is it because there are no pretty people on campus? I will lighten things up in Cambridge. You need me for several reasons:

1. After seeing the movie, *Legally Blonde*, I wanted to be Elle Wood. Like me, she has a sunny disposition because she came from a sunny state. I am not from California, but I am from Florida, which has abundant sunshine year round. I have seen *Legally Blonde*, the follow-up movie, *Legally Blonde: Red, White, and Blonde* many, *many* times, and the Broadway production of *Legally Blonde- The Musical*. Elle and I are so much alike we could be twins…and you accepted her and look how brilliant she turned out to represent Harvard! I even played the part of Elle for Orlando's summer theatre stage production of *Legally Blonde- The Musical* because not only do I look so much like Elle, but I also act like her, too. It is so uncanny how much we resemble each other. You just need an Elle walking around your campus to lighten everyone's mood, which my high school sorority sisters have told me I do at our highly populated high school. People would be excited to see Elle again on campus and they would turn their heads straining to see if it is really her. Thinking they did see her, they would smile. You need more smiles at Harvard. Like

a B-12 shot, I think it would have students, professors, and Cambridgenites take notice of your university because y'all need something or someone to make your campus light up. This would be really good positive publicity for a school that just seems too serious and dour. No one looks like they are having any fun. Let me do something about that because my personality is infectious.

2. I know you do not give out athletic scholarships, but are you really so full of yourself that you are saying you are paying for the *education* of a scholar-athlete? Isn't that what other schools do but are up front about it? That's where I come in. I cheered all four years at my sunny Florida high school and don't tell me cheerleading isn't a sport! It's been a dream of mine to cheer for Harvard. Offer me an academic scholarship and I'll be the best cheerleader on your squad. I'll bring pep and enthusiasm to your school. You need it. As captain of my high school team and with all our training and athleticism, my girls and guys went to nationals to compete and we won a national title. Now, look at the words in that last sentence: team, training and athleticism, compete, and national title. These words describe any athletic competition. If you took out the word, cheerleader, and replaced it, with let's say, volleyball or any other athletic contest, it would all be the same. Cheerleading is a sport! Therefore, I think I would fit in with your cheer squad and bring much needed cheerleading attention to your school because currently I don't see you having any and you need some. If everything is so great over there, why haven't I heard about your cheerleading team? Don't

you see? You need me. I'll make people take notice and smile even with your dreary weather.

3. Commoner, Kate Middleton, found her prince at St. Andrews. I need to hurry up and be accepted so, I may, too, have a shot at John Bouvier Kennedy "Jack" Schlossberg. His last year at Harvard Law School is coming up and this is another dream I have had for years. Like my mother and her John-John Kennedy generation, I have been wanting to meet and marry a Kennedy. He is hot. Once you see my picture, you will know what a cute couple we will make. Not only was I cheerleader captain, but Homecoming Queen. *Queen*! Let's make this happen since he is America's only royalty and I have a queen title. He won't know what hit him. I am in such high demand, I am currently turning down dates at my school because I am booked until next Fall before I leave home. Every red-blooded male wants a date with Elle Wood. But I would make room for John-John Schlossberg. He is the new McDreamy!

4. My grades are right in the middle of the grading curve but my IQ is 119, just like President John F. Kennedy, which means I have potential, right? But it also means I am not overly cocky or act like a smart *** because I don't value grades more than cheerleading. You have enough people making good grades. I am your gal to make them look good because I am right smack in the middle while they are trying to prove they are the smartest in the room. Not me. I want to major in popularity. I am your future Homecoming Queen. *Queen*! Because I will smile at everyone even if the Harvard types don't smile

much… they won't forget me. Together you and I can do this and make Harvard a happier place. I'll make you so proud you accepted me when I become Mrs. John Bouvier Kennedy Schlossberg!

See you in September!
Sunny Day

My College Admissions Essay
by
Bill Overdew

IN ORDER FOR THE ADMISSIONS STAFF OF OUR COLLEGE TO GET TO KNOW YOU, THE APPLICANT, BETTER, WE ASK THAT YOU ANSWER THE FOLLOWING QUESTION: ARE THERE ANY SIGNIFICANT EXPERIENCES YOU HAVE HAD, OR ACCOMPLISHMENTS YOU HAVE ACHIEVED THAT HAVE HELPED TO DEFINE YOU AS A PERSON?

While an Explorer Scout and to obtain my Invention Badge, I single handedly designed a baby stroller attached to a low-riding tricycle so Mom or Dad can get a workout while strolling around with their offspring. In one day, I built my invention after school while babysitting my neighbor's three month old, so when I say single handedly, it is not an exaggeration, as I was holding a baby in the other.

I speak fluent Mongolian and teach a Mongolian-to-English translation class on the world wide web. Mostly my students only care about learning obscenities commonly used in the English language. I was awarded Best All-Around Athlete every year of high school. Because I was more talented than any other high school athlete before I even reached high school, they also gave me that *same* high school award during my 7th and 8th grade years.

I never have to ask a female for a date. I keep a calendar on my Facebook page and girls sign up on the *Date Bill Overdew* site. I am booked every weekend through 2023 with some weekday nights pending. People steal my profile picture to "catfish" for their own dates in other states. I make and bake my own Pop-Tarts. I always begin singing, with accuracy, middle "C". I can play by ear Queen's "Bohemian Rhapsody" on the French horn. I can make Minute Rice in fifty seconds. I read the unabridged version of *War and Peace (1,225 pages),* and the entire Harry Potter series (*1,427 pages*) in one sleepless night.

I have helped orphans in India, been told that Hawking's greatest written work was plagiarized from my 6th grade science paper. I can outrun a 1975 AMC Gremlin. I breed and will show my Lagotto Romagnolo, a new entry, in this year's Westminster Dog Show. During my most recent hike on the Oregon Trail, I surgically and successfully removed a ruptured hernia from our guide using only your basic camping tools.

I am the subject of many PBS documentaries. I wrote the book, *The Brief History of Dots and Polka Dots.* Tom Petty called me the night before he died. I bought an oil painting at a local garage sale and when it began to peel, there was another painting behind it: the stolen *"Congregation Leaving the Reformed Church in Neunen" (1884-85)* by Vincent Van Gogh. I returned it to Van Gogh Museum in Amsterdam. I won three consecutive Xtreme Bull Riding titles at the Reno Rodeo, the "wildest, richest rodeo in the West."

My intricate cross-stitch American samplers hang with the earliest known samplers (from Plymouth Colony around 1645) in the National Museum of American History. *Master Chef* begged me to participate in their 2015 television season. I once played golf with Rory McIlroy and beat him. I have the private home number of Christopher Wray,

Director of the FBI. We speak on a monthly basis. I am nominated for the new special Academy Award for Background Day Players at the upcoming 2019 Oscars for my outstanding performance of a blind man in a mob scene in the movie, *Vice*. After seeing my acting, the nomination committee created this award for the first time this year.

I hope you will consider my application to attend your fine university. I feel like I have much still to contribute these next few formative years and I would like to make that contribution at your school.

Yours Truly,
Bill Overdew

College Admissions Essay to Brown University
by
Isabelle Ringing

Dear Brown University Admissions,

It has always been my dream to be accepted to Brown University in Providence, Rhode Island. One reason is because John-John Kennedy attended, but mostly I am a big fan of your "Open Curriculum" concept. Why complete a set of core courses when only a few really interest you? I care nothing about being a Renaissance Woman. I don't need to know a little bit about a lot of things. I just want to know a lot about a few things because all I have ever wanted to do in life was to be a baker, most specifically, bake *bread*, and with your idea of letting students have greater freedom to study what we choose and the flexibility to discover what we love, I just know it will work with my personality. I mean who doesn't love bread? Even diabetics wish they could eat more of it. It is the "staff of life", right? A very basic food that supports life and is a metaphor for life…thick and crusty on the outside but soft and spongy in the middle, unless you have a hard six-pack like Zac Ephron.

For instance in your *Africana Studies*, I'd like to only take a class on specializing in the making and baking of pita bread. I hope there is an old recipe for that. I know a lot about bread but not everything so, I could expand my interest about the ancient Greek barley bread– or solon – that was baked for feast days and hopefully found in your *Anthropology* course. In your *Eastern Asian Studies,* I can concentrate on China's traditional bread, mantou. Did you know you steam or deep fry the dough made from wheat flour

and it is eaten as an alternative staple to rice. I want
that recipe, too. In Egypt they have flatbread, similar
to pita, but it's baked with whole-wheat flour in
scorching-hot ovens in Cairo's bustling markets.
Surely they will cover that in your course, *Egyptology
and Assyriology*. *Ass*yriology? Whoa, wait a minute,
you should change that name of study. Although,
since it is the study of language, history, and
antiquities of Assyria and if they discuss the baking
tools of the Assyrians, I'm in! Call it what you will.
Just help me build my bread recipe repertoire. I did
hear they ate bread baked in the shape of large
pancakes on a convex metal surface. I could dig that!
And *French and Francophone Studies* – ooh, la, la!
Nothing like French croissants or crepes. But, hey, I
don't get offended hanging around Francophones. I
am not biased. I walked in the LBGTV parade last
year. I even carried a rainbow flag. I have lots of
different kinds of friends. I mean, really? Who is
phobic of the French?

I can stretch myself with your *Applied
Mathematics* because I'd be applying math to my
cooking like using correct measurements both dry and
liquid, which I already know, *duh*. That one might be
an easy "A". *Chemistry* would be helpful knowing
about the right mixture and baking temperatures for
all this newfound knowledge. And your *Business*
course or *Entrepreneurship and Organizations* study
would be perfect for learning how to start my own
bread business. Maybe they will help me come up
with a great name for my business. I've been
throwing around *Half-Baked*; *Pat-A-Cake-Baker's
Man*; *Hot Crossed Buns (*thinking of Zac Ephron
again on that one*); Baker's Dozen; The Butcher, The*

*Baker, The Candlestick Maker (*but I don't know how to do those other things*); or Bake Up A Storm.*

Personally, your *Behavioral Decision Sciences* interest me greatly. I'd love to get to the root of why I love baking bread so much, as long as finding out *why* doesn't make me depressed or crazy. Your *Independent Concentration* would help me stay focused on my goals, I'm sure.

What I like about your allowing students to tailor their interest keep me from having to take courses like these at Brown: *The Classics, Comparative Literature, Development Studies,* and *Gender and Sexuality Studies* to make me more well-rounded. As you can see, I am linear – and possess a one-track mind!

Thank goodness for Brown University for <u>catering</u> (pun intended) to the needs of its student body!

I must tell you I won my high school's "Lunchroom Ladies Favorite High School Student" for three out of my four years. The only reason I didn't win all four years was because I was overheard one year making a comment to another student about the cafeteria's homemade rolls that year. They really were disgusting. The rolls were neither good nor nutritious. I came in second place in A. Cisco Bakery's Bake-off my sophomore year, first place in Mazzola's bread category cook-off my junior year, and Sara Lee grand prize winner of my hometown (population 36,549!) county's Southeastern Section of the Girls' Only Junior Division. Yes, thought that would impress you.

Again, I'll be the student you will be glad to have attend your fine university and who you will be proud of for years to come when I learn from the fine professors, chefs, cooks, dough punchers, pastry makers, culinarians, hash slingers, mess sergeants, servants, sous chefs, and others whose baking skills or knowledge of the antiquities used in baking bread are taught at Brown.

Go Bears!
Isabelle Ringing

My College Admissions Essay
by
Fay Slift

IN ORDER FOR THE ADMISSIONS STAFF OF OUR COLLEGE TO GET TO KNOW YOU, THE APPLICANT, BETTER, WE ASK THAT YOU ANSWER THE FOLLOWING QUESTION: ARE THERE ANY SIGNIFICANT EXPERIENCES YOU HAVE HAD, OR ACCOMPLISHMENTS YOU HAVE ACHIEVED THAT HAVE HELPED TO DEFINE YOU AS A PERSON?

Dear Admissions Office,

I am very honored to apply to your fine university and feel, as a student with my interests and talents, I will make a significant contribution.

I do not know how far back you want me to go in my life naming all of my accomplishments but some do lead to my choices in high school.

For instance, beginning with my ballet lessons as a young child, I was cast as one of the young ballerinas in the remake of *White Christmas*, a now defunct Hallmark Christmas special. Remember the little girls at the end of the original movie with Bing Crosby and Rosemary Clooney where they were singing in that extravaganza at the inn for the Colonel? Do you recall those three little girls who danced on stage with them (on toe!) and helped light the Christmas tree at the end of the movie. I was to be one of those three in this new production. But, alas, they lost funding for the project.

From that experience, I loved being on stage and decided I wanted to dance in high school, college, and after. In high school, I successfully was chosen to be

the lead female in *Hamlet – The Musical* (I was to
play the part of Ophelia because of my dramatic
suicide performance) which was critiqued by the
Balderdash Sentinel Entertainment Editor: "Miss Slift
portrays the misunderstood Ophelia perfectly in
Hamlet – The Musical because I certainly was
confused the whole time she danced on stage." See? I
was perfect for the part.

I speak flawless French and plan to dance in Paris
when I graduate. Well, it's not really French words. I
use American words with a French dialect. But I hear
the Parisians speak English so well, I do not need to
learn French anyway. Should I need to, if I drive out
to the countryside and become lost, I will just take my
iPhone with me and consult the English to French
translation app if they have service. If not, I can mime
my way to help them understand my predicament
because I would like to minor in acting while
attending college, although I only joined my high
school theater group, Dramarama, my Senior year. It
was here I was cast the as one of the swans in the
production of *Swan Lake – The Drama*. I had to peck
at the Diva Swan throughout the performance to show
jealousy or something like that. I never really
understood my director's directions. That's why it
will be my *minor*. Dance will still be my *major*.

I was President of the Bon Jovi Society in my high
school. I was the mascot for our football team and ran
on the field to serve the players Gatorade during time-
outs. Once, because of my beautiful ballerina feet
(long and patrician), I was chosen by my nail salon,
This Little Piggy Nail Salon, to have my toenails
photographed for an advertisement for the local paper
after one technician artfully painted my big toenail
with our high school's crest before the Junior-Senior

prom. That's intricate work! I wore sandals to the prom just so it could be seen. So not only have I danced on stage and acted on stage, I am also a model.

I carved *by myself* my wood recorder which I play at birthday party gigs for elementary school children's birthdays. I gets lots of compliments when I play, "In A Gadda Da Vida", "Stairway to Heaven", "YMCA", and "Supercalifragilisticexpialidocious".

While in 4-H, I won second runner-up in the cow pull contest sponsored by the "Got Milk?" campaign. And I'm sure you know what we were pulling. My *bucket* list is to win it this Fall before I leave for college. Pun intended.

I type twenty-six words per minute with just a few mistakes. Because of this skill, I applied for a job at the Barbie Lands A Job Staffing Company. They told me they would call me when they needed me, but I haven't heard from them…yet. It's been over a year. And, have you noticed, I have not misspelled a word in this document, although it's taken me two hours to make it perfect.

Well, enough about me. I am well rounded, love nature (cow contest), a prissy girl (dancing, modeling, and acting), but willing to work hard (temp agency).

I would love to be included at your prestigious university.

Many thanks,
Fay Slift

The Useful, the Useless, and the Ridiculous
The college courses are real, but the students are not

Dear Mrs. St. John,

Beginning this summer, I am attending college early to get the lay of land - all things college has to offer but with an early start before tons of students arrive in the Fall.

I have not decided on a major as of yet and want to ease into college but still obtain college credit. I have just completed my registration and been accepted into the following classes. I'd like to get your input.

Here are the course descriptions:

<u>Language and Literature</u>

Just like at the University of California at Berkeley, my college is offering **Arguing with Judge Judy:** The description reads - Popular 'Logic' on TV Judge Shows: Ever felt like the plaintiffs on TV judge shows have some pretty questionable logic? This class addresses that subject directly, allowing students to dissect courtroom excuses just like Judge Judy.

<u>History</u>

While Occidental College in Los Angeles offers this class, I can get credit for it also at my new school. It is entitled: **The Phallus**: Explore the role this part of the male body has played in society from the early, often sexist works of Freud to newer feminist theories.

<u>Sociology, Psychology and Anthropology</u>

I feel lucky to take a course like this one this summer because it is also offered at MIT. **The Lucifer Effect**: Understanding How Good People Turn Evil: This course examines a question that many people ask themselves–how can good people do bad things?

I appreciate any input you might send my way. Maybe taking one of these courses will spark something in my choice of a major.

Sincerely,

Marsha Mellow

****

Dear Mrs. St. John,
I am looking forward to college and even more so now since I found these courses that seem interesting. Who knew these programs of study would be so intriguing! I mean, WOW! I can take them online through my community college. At least I hope so because they have caught my attention.
I don't know what to major in but after enrolling in these, I might. And, boy, will it look good on my transcript that I received credit from these leading institutions. I might even transfer there if I like the course.

As a Science major, I found this offering at the University of California, Irvine. And it's a science credit:

The Science of Superheroes. The description reads, "While it might sound like fun and games, this course takes superheroes as a means to teach students real lessons about physics." This may be the only way I could pass physics since I like superheroes and have seen all the Avengers movies.

I need to take a philosophy class and liked the title of this one:

The Simpsons and Philosophy. My course catalogue states, "While the Simpsons may appear to be just good entertainment, this course shows the deeper philosophical issues under all those 'd'ohs.'" And to think this course is also offered at The University of California at Berkeley. WOW!

This next course is listed under technology:

The Strategy of Starcraft: "Fans of this game say it's one of the most difficult to master, but this course at University of California at Berkeley aims to help students learn the game better through lessons from one its creators." Can you believe I might have the opportunity to take this course? Remember how many times I stayed in the hall and was late to your class talking to the technology teacher about this? He always wrote notes for me to come in late without penalty. Thank you, Mrs. St. John for taking his late-to-class hall pass.

Anyway, wanted to keep you abreast of my course selection at my community college, should they accept me. You and the tech teacher, I forgot his name, were my favorite teachers in high school.

Sincerely,
Ty Tannic

P.S. Could you write a letter of recommendation as required by my community college?

****
****

Dear Mrs. St. John,

I didn't think I was college material because of my English grades all throughout high school but now that we just graduated, all my girlfriends are talking about going off to school, getting letters of recommendations for sorority rush, and plain just leaving me behind, I think I wanna go to college.

I was talking to Ty Tannic who is going to junior college and he suggested that maybe I should do the same. I was looking through the course catalogue of Rumford Junior College and saw that I can take courses in the comfort of my own home while watching my favorite soap opera during the day. I can't miss *General Hospital*. My mother started watching it before I was born and I was brought up on it because I couldn't interrupt her watching the soap. So, I sat there watching it with her. Maybe that's why I love television so much and like this online course.

Who knew colleges offered classes like these? In Popular Culture, which focuses on phenomena and icons, this course catches a lot of guff for its seemingly trivial subject matter, but I like it: <u>Oprah Winfrey: The Tycoon</u>. "This course gives students a chance to delve deep into the life of one of the most successful and recognizable women in the world."

Wait a minute! Oh, it says it is no longer offered as an online course at the University of Illinois at Urbana. Bummer! Well, I'll just have to find another icon. Besides, I think I have read everything there is to know on Oprah in my *STAR, People,* and *InTouch* magazines.

My mama keeps telling me to save my money from my part-time job at the Hot Diggity Dog Drive-Thru. Maybe I should take this course. I can get it through Alfred U. Where in the heck is that? But I could make my mama proud. It's called: <u>Tightwaddery, or The Good Life on a Dollar a Day</u>. "While the title might elicit some laughs, this course offers some sage advice on breaking the bonds of consumerism and fighting back against the status quo. And if that isn't part of a well-rounded college education, then what is?"

Mrs. St. John, what is consumerism? Even though I live at home, I wonder if I really can live on a dollar a day, even if I have to paint my nails myself and color my own hair. I've still gotta have my Big Mac and Diet Coke occasionally!

Well, I just hope I can get into college. It says I need a letter of recommendation. Do you mind writing one? If you need to know my high school activities, I was third alternate for second soprano in Girls Chorus for two years but I never got to sing because no one ever got sick, except for Brook Trout, first soprano, so when second alternate took her place, that's as close as I got. So, really, I was, for a while, first alternate for the second soprano position and you could mention that.

You and the Girls Chorus teacher were my favorite teachers in high school.

Hope you are doing well.

Thank you,

Polly Wannacracker

High School Timed Test Essays

Frankenstein Timed Essay

Themes are the fundamental and often universal ideas explored in a literary work. Here are several we discussed in class while reading *Frankenstein* by Mary Shelley: dangerous knowledge, family, alienation, ambition, sublime nature, monstrosity, and secrecy. Choose one of the above and during this seventy minute timed essay, defend your choice with examples from the text in your book.

The Monster Mash
by
Simon Sess

First let me say, Victor Frankenstein, as a university student, was an overachiever. What good did it do him? Victor – calm down. Relax, dude. This really should be the lesson learned in the ~~movie~~ story. The End. But I have to write for another twenty-five minutes. I know you are asking, "Why not seventy minutes?" Because I had to think about it first, obviously. So for forty-five minutes I contemplated saying just what I said in my first few sentences. I really am a man of few words, but you want us to write, write, and write! Ok, let me think a bit more…

Also in the first forty-five minutes, I had to sharpen my pencil twice as I kept dropping it on the floor and the lead broke. Once while thinking, I chewed on my number two pencil and didn't realize that I was chewing the lead part and that was one of the times it broke off. So, all that took some time because the line to the pencil sharpener was at least three people deep ahead of me, and they were obviously in no hurry, either. One person, Gerry Tall, visited the pencil sharpener three times while I was ~~goofing off~~ plotting.

Everyone thinks the monster is named Frankenstein but in reality it belongs to Dr. Victor Frankenstein who brought him to life *and* made him ugly, I might add. Why did he make him so ugly? At eight feet tall and with all that new (but previously dead tissue – but new to him) he could have made him handsome so he wouldn't be rejected by society. That was just plain stupid. When you build something for the first time one would want to have it looked upon as a piece of art and yet what does this doctor do? He gives his creation a bad reputation right off the bat.

Let's face it. The monster was grotesque from the unnatural way he was put together with the secret animation mix of stolen body parts and strange chemicals. Well, stealing something from someone else will cause Karma to come back and bite you. In this case, it sure did. And not only did the monster suffer rejection, Victor's idea of trying to create a master race by stitching rotting corpses into a superhuman giant, made him suffer, too. But that's what he gets from being arrogant, obsessed, and thinking he was intellectually superior to his contemporaries. Victor, you need to chill out, buddy.

Rhoda Mule, who thinks she is so smart, always tries to come in first finishing whatever is assigned. She usually gets all the answers correct on our tests and she finishes fast. What a nerd. She is now reading a book of her choice (approved by our teacher) to pass the rest of the time for our timed essay. I guess that means time is almost up, but does it? Since she always likes to finish fast, maybe she just finished fast so she could one up everybody or to pull a prank on us slow folks. Whatever, I can't stand her. I asked her out once and she turned me down. She turned *me* down. She said I wasn't smart enough for her and that she had grand plans to go to some Ivy League school. Who cares how much ivy a school has on its brick walls anyway?

Anyway, Victor was left isolated with his uptight and deranged thoughts and his failure as the monster will never fit in, so what was the point? Oh, yeah. Mary Shelley wrote this story while on opium. Well, now: there's another theme of the book. Don't take drugs and write. Well, I am *supposed* to say, "Don't take drugs at all." But I do hope the Georgia legislature is going to legalize the medical marijuana bill because I can't function without it and to get even a little bit might help me because it's the only way I can endure school now.

Maybe if Victor, the monster, and Mary Shelley had just taken marijuana instead, everyone would have just calmed down and all this wouldn't have….

TIME!

Julius Caesar Timed Essay

This timed test will have you identifying the themes, ambition, and conflict, found in Shakespeare's play, *Julius Caesar*. Give examples in dialogue and action of these two characteristics found in all three men: Caesar, Brutus, and Cassius. You have seventy minutes.

Hey, Jealousy!
by
Anne Teak

A few of Caesar's friends start to find him annoying, but really it boils down to being jealous of him. The play, *Julius Caesar* by Edward Shakespeare, takes place a very long time ago in Rome, Italy, where you see all those partially crushed columns, sculptures with their heads, arms, or hands broken off, and stadiums that are crumbling more each day like in those gladiator movies where the young men wear a loincloth to cover their private parts, but show their muscular, no-haired (thank goodness, because hairy chests are gross!) bare chests, and six-pack abs, yet the older men wear robes that they call togas which I first learned about in the movie *Animal House* during their toga party scene. Both young and old alike wear sandals with straps going up their legs that help to hold the sandal in place because they really didn't measure your foot back then and just sold or made you sandals that were close in size for you to wear. That's why there was a need for leather straps to hold the open toe sandal in place on your foot so it wouldn't come loose and cause you stub your toe, because that would really hurt.

But Caesar is going to get hurt anyway. He didn't get hurt during the war. He came home unharmed from that. It's when he returns home a hero that his friends turned on him. But he was also so full of himself about his triumphs at war that he did not heed the warning signs. Well, there were really no visual signs. He should have paid attention to a stranger in Rome who told him to "Beware the Ides of March." The Ides of March is March 15th. Ides means a day falling roughly in the middle of each month. Sometimes the middle of a month might be the thirteenth, so it is not always on the fifteenth of every month like in March.

I always associated that date bringing bad luck, and then one turns right around and on March 17th it's a good luck day because of it being St. Patrick's Day, which is a happy time with happy leprechauns dancing in the streets at a St. Patrick's Day Parade like in Dublin, Georgia or Savannah. Everyone is wearing Kelly green – and not the green of envy, either – and most people at the parades are happy because they are smashed from green beer and wearing strings of beads and sparkly top hats and carrying four-leaf clovers for good luck, so maybe that is the reason there is even a St. Patrick's Day at all: something to finally have people feel good about something around that time of month especially after the downer of Caesar being stabbed by his own friends.

Our teacher told us we have twenty minutes left.

I really know St. Patrick's Day is about the saint, Patrick, who ministered Christianity in Ireland during the fifth century, but why did they choose March 17th?

Caesar was caught up in his own hype and his friends, Cassius and Brutus become concerned and jealous. Really, it was Cassius more than Brutus. But Brutus hangs around to see how the revenge they plan will play out. Caesar is so full of himself, he doesn't even listen to his wife, Calpurnia, when she tells him about a dream, well I'd say nightmare, she had about his being murdered in town and begs him not to go. So, arrogant Caesar has had two warnings about the Ides of March, but he goes anyway and is a dead man walking.

Ambition and conflict blind all three men, so...

Teacher says ten minutes left...

I have to hurry and tell the best parts where Brutus ends up stabbing Caesar as the last of all the conspirators and it becomes the final blow that kills him but before he dies, Caesar says, "Et tu, Brute" which is Latin. They all spoke Latin back then. And I don't see how that is even a language given it doesn't even have all the letters of our alphabet in their Greek Alphabet. Our alphabet has twenty-six letters and Greek/Latin has Alpha, Beta, Gamma, Delta, Epsilon, Zeta, Eta, Theta, Iota, Kappa, Lambda, Mu, Nu, Xi, Omicron, Pi, Rho, Sigma, Tau, Upsilon, Phi, Chi, Psi, Omega. Which is only twenty-four letters. I know this because my older sister just pledged Tri-Delt at the University of Georgia. She taught me all the Greek letters and the song that goes with it.

And then there's the quote, "Great Caesar's Ghost!", which...

TIME!

Henry David Thoreau and Transcendentalism Timed Essay

Transcendentalism is a philosophical movement found in the eastern United States and developed in the late 1820s and 1830s. Transcendentalists are strong believers in the power of the individual. It came about as a reaction to protest against the general state of intellectualism and spirituality of the time and focuses primarily on personal freedom and empiricism – which philosophically speaking is the knowledge that comes only or primarily from sensory experiences.

Henry David Thoreau, one of the best known Transcendentalists, said, "I went to the woods because I wished to live deliberately, to front only the essential facts of life, and see if I could not learn what it had to teach, and not, when I came to die, discover that I had not lived."

Prompt: *Describe what Henry David Thoreau learned from his experience "On Walden's Pond." You have seventy minutes.*

On Walden's Lake
by
C. Shell

In our American Literature class we learned that Thoreau went into the woods in 1845. He lived in a simple cabin for two years and two months, which he built on Walden's Pond. I suppose he was an environmentalist before his time. But the pond isn't really a pond at all. Near Concord, Massachusetts, this pond was really a lake surrounded by a forest. If he's so smart, wouldn't he know the difference?

I mean, that whole Transcendentalist movement was adopted by Harvard University. Aren't they supposed to be some of the smartest people alive? This whole-leaving-society-to-find-yourself-in- nature is kinda crazy – like Ted Kaczynski crazy. Ted was a smart Harvard man and didn't like the way society was going. He built a "little cabin in the woods" like the song says and look what he did...

Ted Kaczynski was either crazy before he left, or became that way after he set up shop in his makeshift home. Without much socialization, I think I would go crazy, too! No fashion magazines? No Pinterest? No telephone? No Netflix? I mean, how would one exist? They are both nuts.

And I guess that was what they were eating a lot of, too: nuts. I bet they both had to fight with squirrels over them during the winter. At least Thoreau went up to his "little cabin in the woods" to commune with nature. My mother told me in confidence, but I am sharing with you now, that my grandmother went to Woodstock in the 1960s to commune 'au natural'. Doesn't that mean being natural – like where the word nature comes from? So, my granny was a naturalist, too.

I don't think Kaczynski had a pond, though. At least Thoreau could have caught and cooked fish. Since he wanted to learn more through nature, he probably learned how to clean the fish he caught and maybe he had some special recipes he could use to make each fish dish different.

The clock says I have twelve more minutes.

How many ways can you bake fish over an open fire? And what vegetables are you eating? Dandelions? Ugh! So much for learning something new and different. I'd be learning that I didn't like dandelions. Now there's a self-taught lesson.

I might like to take a vacation for a day without company but over two years? No, thank you. I'd get homesick without my family around, like in the movie *Home Alone*. Kevin eventually missed his family although he had to learn that the hard way. Maybe Thoreau was also writing about what he might miss and what he didn't miss. I didn't get to read all of it because I was at gymnastics really late all week because region finals are next month and I...

TIME!

Hamlet Timed Essay

The Tragedy of Hamlet, Prince of Denmark depicts Prince Hamlet seeking revenge against his uncle, Claudius, who has murdered Hamlet's father in order to seize his throne while marrying Hamlet's mother. Most people know the play only as Hamlet, a tragedy written by Shakespeare. Point of View is a literary term meaning how the writer wants to convey the experience to the reader. First-person point of view is allowing a character to tell the story.

Choose a soliloquy (you may use your book to duplicate the verse into your essay) but it must be rewritten in first person point of view and in your own words. This exercise will help me know you understand Shakespeare's written words. You have seventy-five minutes.

These Lovely Bones

by

Bess Twiches

I bet everyone is going to write about the "To be or not to be..." scene. Not me. I find Hamlet's finding his former court jester's skull fascinating. Yorick is dead and his skull is exhumed by the first gravedigger in Act Five, Scene One. How in the heck Hamlet knows without a doubt that it's his court jester is beyond me, because when watching Mel Gibson's movie version of *Hamlet*, it was just a bare skull. So it was buried with the other members of court in their own graveyard, it still seems impossible to identify him by his skull. The rest of the body was not attached.

Here is the play's version of what Hamlet said after finding someone who must have played an important role in his upbringing: "Alas, poor Yorick! I knew him, Horatio; a fellow of infinite jest, of most excellent fancy; he hath borne me on his back a thousand times; and now, how abhorred in my imagination it is! My gorge rises at it. Here hung those lips that I have kissed I know not how oft. Where be your gibes now? Your gambols? Your songs? Your flashes of merriment, that were wont to set the table on a roar?" (*Hamlet*, V.i)

Here is how I understand it:

"Yo, Yorick! Poor guy. Dead as a doornail. But I recognize you. Are you listening to me, Horatio? You said you wanted to come along with me to look after me so I wouldn't do something crazy like killing myself like Ophelia did. And to think she drowned herself…in a foot of water. What's that all about? Horatio – are you paying attention? I knew this guy. He was one of our court jesters. One of my favorites, really. He was an excellent jester, too. He'd perform cartwheels and pretend to fall after every one. I laughed myself silly. He let me ride on his back like a donkey and would bray. That was hilarious. I gave him one of those idiotic jester hats for Christmas one year. The next year I gave him a toy jester with bells attached to a stick. What harebrained gifts those were.

He performed great mimes of monkeys and elephants or getting marbles stuck up his nose. Once he really did get a marble stuck up his nose. We had to shake him upside down to have it fall out. He was a one-man variety show. Daddy made him eat stuff before he put it in his own mouth to make sure his food wasn't poisoned. And look how that turned out. Somehow it got past Yorick. All it took was once for my poor daddy!

If my daddy was living in this century he would want to eat and watch TV at the same time like many families do at dinner time. I say this because he would always have a jester perform while he ate his meals and would laugh and laugh. Once he got a chicken wishbone stuck in his throat, and luckily my Christmas gift to Yorick of the jester-on-a-stick helped un-lodge it. Yorick was so faithful.

I must turn away. I can't look any longer at this skull without a body. Although I must say, I do need a paperweight for my office. Maybe Yorick's skull, since he was a dwarf, will do the trick. And Yo! Yorick will get to do another trick – a continuous trick- holding my papers so they will not fly away. His legacy will live on.

When I see you now, Yorick, hey, Horatio come back here and listen, I think of that merry song you always sang to me when my parents wanted to be alone. You kept me company as I searched the castle halls and rooms for them as I thought they were playing hide-and-go-seek. You sang that meaningless song with the words, "Aye, der buoy with the bonny blew eyes. Follow me for yer nice surprise." I never understood what that meant exactly with your heavy Scottish brogue, which never changed, BTW, even as long as you lived in Denmark. Horatio – don't walk away while I am fondly remembering this fool!

You were a great babysitter, Yorick. Your parental kisses comforted me when I was sick or you could make me laugh to get over my tears. You really were like a parent to me and I will keep your skull with me as long as I live, which (*spoiler alert*!) may not be too much longer."

Well, there you have it. First person point of view from a scene in Hamlet.

Gosh, I can't believe I finished ahead everybody. I've never done that before. Everyone else around me is writing furiously and I've still got one minute left before our teacher calls...

TIME!

Robert Frost's "The Road Not Taken" Timed Essay

The main theme of the poem written on our classroom board by Robert Frost is that human beings are confronted with and ultimately defined by the choices they make. This main idea in the poem is universal, so for the next seventy minutes, describe one of your own personal crossroads in the essay and the choice you made after confronting your own fork in the road. Incorporate lines or ideas from the poem.

My Road Not Taken
by
Y. Bother

The poem, "The Road Not Taken" is supposed to be a telling tale, and yet Robert Frost does not tell us anything about his journey. He just tells us about his two choices staring him right in the face and how he stood for a long time looking at the paths. He followed as far as his eyes could see both paths to help him with his decision. He finally chose one.

So, why did he call them roads? Or a path? Neither was a path or road after all because there was still grass on both – just higher on one than the other. If the grass wasn't worn down to the dirt from previous hikers, how could he tell it was even a way to walk on at all? How did *he know* the grass wanted to be walked on? The poem said, "**Because it was grassy and wanted wear**"? What was that all about it? And Frost mentioned that he took the unused path because it was "just as fair". How did he know that? He hadn't walked that walk. There might be bears and snakes hanging from the trees to frighten him. Bears and hanging snakes would have frightened me.

The clock in my room tells me another twenty minutes.

Well, it doesn't actually tell me. You know what I mean. When an inanimate object takes on personal qualities that is called some literary term I am supposed to know. So, even though I don't know the name, I thought I would throw that in here to let you know I was listening to part of what you were saying and hope that I get some extra points for bringing it up.

The third stanza said he didn't turn back to return to the fork in the road. Why would he? There is another poem that we read that mentioned one can never go home again. Maybe Frost read that poem, too. I guess that's why we study literature – so we can learn something from it. But sometimes the words are so old like that I don't know what they 'sayeth'.

My stomach is growling. It must be time for lunch, which means, I guess, that the darn test is almost over. I hope Derrie Anne Connecticut doesn't hear it growling. Last year I invited her to go to the county fair with me because my mother and her mother played bridge together, and my mother kept asking her mother if she was seeing anyone, and her mother didn't ever answer my mother the whole time that day and even the next time they played bridge at some old woman's house she kept asking if I could call her Derrie Anne up sometime and invite her out. Her mother finally said "Yes" and when I did call, Derrie Anne didn't answer the phone but her sister did and finally gave the call to her and we talked for a whole thirty-two seconds (I counted on my watch) and that's when I asked her out and she hesitated, but with the long silence on the other end of the phone, I could hear her mother yell, "Just say yes and be done with it and never go out with him again," and so she said "Yes." So, we went to the fair and she later she told me she got separated from me when she went to the bathroom and got lost, so she got another ride home.

A girl in the hall from our teacher's last class said that we would be writing about this poem. She said she read that Frost once said he didn't mean anything by writing this poem: he just wrote a poem. And a friend of mine, a big Jerry Seinfeld fan, said he heard Seinfeld say, "Sometimes the road less traveled is less traveled for a reason." I wonder if Frost felt this way.

I am also supposed to tell about some crossroad I came upon.

Since I am supposed to reference a crossroads of my own, I'll mention I was thinking about asking Anetta Fish, to the Junior-Senior last year. I couldn't make up my mind because of my bad experience with Derrie Anne, so I waited and waited and then didn't ask her after all. On the way back from the dance, I heard that she went with another guy to the prom and threw up in the limousine on his tux, so I was glad that I didn't take that *road*!

TIME!

"The Raven" by Edgar Allan Poe and its Symbolism
Timed Essay

*Prompt: "The Raven" is a narrative poem
by American writer, Edgar Allan Poe. First published
in January 1845, the poem is often noted for its
musicality, stylized language, and supernatural
atmosphere. In this timed essay, you will have
seventy-five minutes to explore: what is a narrative
poem and what literary devices does Poe use to
create his supernatural atmosphere?*

Caw!
by
May Bellen

My first thought about our reading "The Raven"
and when I heard that bird keep saying, "Nevermore,
nevermore," was if one wrote raven backwards and
misspelled it, it would almost be the word *never*.
Think about it…n-e-v-a-r and n-e-v-e-r. Pretty close,
right? Maybe Poe did that on purpose. Maybe he was
a poor speller. Maybe he didn't have an editor that
checked his work. Anyway, it was just a thought.

And what is that called anyway when a word reads
the same backward or forward? It begins with a "p".
Like in the word *racecar* or *radar*. I think it's palli-
something. Oh, well. Maybe Poe made that talking
bird a raven so that it would be that literary term. Or
maybe he was so out of it that it came to him in a bad
dream. He had an awful life and I think he tried to
escape it with drugs or whatever. He might have been
bitten by a rabid dog when they found him dead in the
streets instead of dying from alcohol poisoning. What
an awful thing to happen to such a creative writer.

Ravens are black birds and because they are black, I guess he used the raven to have a conversation with. Black is associated with death and the supernatural. That's why people wear black to funerals. So having a black bird makes sense. But why couldn't it be a crow? And what is the difference between the two? Or why can't a black bird be *called* a blackbird? I mean, why all the names for these black birds? Who is paying attention to the slightest detail among them? I'm really thinking Poe used the raven because he is going with the palli-word thingy.

Why is Poe, our narrator (hence a narrative poem), so sad and deciding to talk to some bird that just happened to land on his open windowsill? And was the window open? Was it hot? You know, Poe once lived in Boston for a time and it gets cold up there. I know. I visited my aunt there once who is professor of American English Literature at Boston College. (wink, wink – brownie point?)

Whenever I break up with a boyfriend and feel sad, my parents just tell me to get over it. There is always something better around the corner. What is wrong with Poe? I am sure his parents and guardian told him the same thing, but no, he had to go and write another poem, "Annabell Lee" about another girl that he was no longer with. If he keeps dating all these girls that die, you can forget I'd ever go out with him if I were ever introduced to him. Forgettaboutit. I don't have a death wish.

And of all the things for the raven to say, "Nevermore." Gimme a break. That in no way sounds like "caw." I mean, really. How could he ever mistake a real human word for "caw"?

I swear, the smartest person in our class has put his head down on his desk like for the last thirty minutes, which tells me he has finished his timed essay, which means, I guess, that it is almost time to stop.

To prove it is a supernatural poem, Poe uses words like "quoth", "sayeth", even the word "December", because it is cold up there in Boston and it makes you stay inside and you get cabin fever; "velvet" which is old material and I am sure would be dirty and dusty making it gross and stinky in that confined space during the winter. Other literary terms that come to mind are…

TIME!

Romeo and Juliet Timed Essay

Prompt: Much thought has gone into Shakespeare's *Romeo and Juliet* as star-crossed lovers. It is unique among Shakespeare's tragedies because it is fate, not character that seals their doom. Agree or disagree with this statement citing specific scenes and quotations to support your stance. Since this is a timed test, you have 75 minutes to support your case.

Star-Crossed Lovers
by
Helen Highwater

That the great William Shakespeare's famous book, *Romeo and Juliet*, (which I might add is one of my personal favorites) is not so much about it being about character or fate because one could easily agree with that statement or disagree with it. Is it about character? Or is it about fate? The real answer to this statement has a great deal to do with how Shakespeare might have felt about "character" or "fate."

Certainly as the world's most famous writer, Shakespeare himself must have had some profound thoughts on "character" or "fate." What were his feelings about these young people's character? Or does he lean more to the thought that Romeo and Juliet were held captive by their own fate? While other fine books by Shakespeare are also called tragedies, is *Romeo and Juliet*, a book which I enjoyed reading and rereading, really a tragedy?

To prove one point or the other, one must find (by citing) the specific scenes and quotations in *Romeo and Juliet.* But these quotations and scenes are too numerous to mention in this timed essay. If time permits, I will specify them at the end.

There is no reason to believe Shakespeare himself was ever involved in star-crossed activities. He may have been, but our teacher did not provide that information while teaching this book so I cannot argue that point in this paper. If I had that information, I would have provided it here. As I didn't, I cannot. That is OK because this is a timed test and with everything else I have to write about, I doubt I would have had time to put that information in this writing test that we are taking. I mean, it is one thing to talk about Romeo or Juliet's fate as star-crossed lovers but quite another to add that the playwright might have been subjected to fate, also. Who knows?

She did tell us that the musical *West Side Story* is derived from this book by Shakespeare. I remember she showed us that movie and the fire escape symbolized the balcony scene in the *Romeo and Juliet* movie that we also watched. Although it was in black and white, it was pretty good. I don't think Maria (the Juliet character) was really singing in the movie. Her mouth and the words weren't n'sync. I think it was dubbed. Why do we have to watch such old movies? Hasn't there been a new one made in the last fifty years?

I only have ten more minutes until my time is up. Because of the time constraints on this essay, it has been difficult to prove or disprove the statement about character or fate, although it will always be one of my favorite books that we read this year. I wish I had more time because there are so many wonderful references that should be brought up in this paper and I would if…

TIME.

The Great Gatsby Timed Test

This is a timed test to discuss your knowledge of themes in F. Scott Fitzgerald's, *The Great Gatsby*. Give examples. You have seventy minutes. Good luck!

Sex, Drugs, and Alcohol
by
Ellis I. Land

We were told in class to write attention catching titles and first paragraphs. OK, so the title caught your eye. However, there really were no drugs in the story (that I am aware of) but there was more than enough alcohol to make up for it. Sex? Maybe.

Yet, this was one story I enjoyed more than any other story we have read in English so far. These people knew how to party! To think, I always thought old people stories were boring. Not anymore. And I don't think they partied just on the weekends either. Didn't they have to get up and go to work the next morning? I'd like to have friends like these.

Gatsby hosted all these parties just so Daisy, his first girlfriend who is really not good looking enough for Jay, would show up. The parties had bands and music, lots of liquor, lots of dancing, lots of people, lots of food, lots of people jumping in his pool, lots of servers with silver trays, lots of people getting drunk, lots of people bumping into each other, lots of people spilling drinks on each other, lots of hooting and hollering until the sun came up, and lots of interlopers. Jay Gatsby had lots of money to host a lot of these parties.

His parties took place in New York. They are always partying up there like on New Year's Eve when the ball drops. New York must have lots of parties. My grandparents always have the Sirius radio tuned into the Frank Sinatra station. Sometimes when I borrow their car it will be on that station and once I heard Sinatra singing about New York and how it's the city that never sleeps. I'd like to go to New York but my parents won't take me and I don't have enough money or time to visit on my own. This weekend my parents are visiting my mother's sister in South Carolina and I am staying with my buddy, Jimmy D. Locke, and his parents. They are letting him have a party in his basement while they are upstairs. They also have a pool. I should tell everyone to come dressed like people in *The Great Gatsby*. If I take a picture of us dressed like that, will I get extra credit?

Eventually Daisy's cousin, Nick Carraway, moves in next door to Gatsby and goes to all his parties. Gatsby likes that because sometimes Daisy visits her cousin and sees Jay. Uh, oh. I can't believe we read about that. But Daisy's husband has a girlfriend, too. So I guess they are even.

Gatsby got a lot of his money from bootlegging alcohol in the early 1920s during Prohibition. I guess that's another reason he has lots of alcohol at his parties.

My teacher says I have ten minutes left so I better talk about the theme.

I have to say though, I couldn't believe Tom's ugly girlfriend. Couldn't he find a prettier wife and a prettier girlfriend? This was not how I pictured these people in my mind while reading *Sparknotes* to *help* me understand the book. Our class wanted to see the

Leonardo di Caprio version with Jay Z's music, but since we saw the original movie, the only person I knew in that movie was Robert Redford and the rest of the people were not attractive.

I know my *brainiac* friends are going to say otherwise, but I think the theme is about…

TIME!

Dr. Jekyll and Mr. Hyde Timed Essay

Prompt: Of all the books we read in class this year, for this exercise, write a persuasive paper on a book of your choice. Remember to use as many of the eight persuasive techniques we studied in class: Appeal to Authority. Important people or experts can make your argument seem more convincing; Using reliable research can help your argument seem convincing, Appeal to Reason, Appeal to Emotion, Appeal to Trust, Appeal by Plain Spokesperson or Celebrity Spokesperson Testimony, Appeal to Act Fast and Jumping on the Bandwagon, Appeal by using a Rhetorical Question (and don't ask me during the test what that is again!), and finally Appeal through Repetition (I am not saying that a Rhetorical Question is again – get it?)

The Shadow Knows
by
Sid Down

I am a massive *The Shadow* comic book fan; good and evil is something I know all too well. I mean, I like reading comic books. You can learn a lot from comic books or even cartoons. How many times did you hear classic music on Bugs Bunny? Lots. This is why I can relate to our book we read for class, *Dr. Jekyll and Mr. Hyde.*

This time our teacher didn't show us a movie about it. I like it when she shows us the movie version. I get more out of it when I see the movie version. It fills in the gaps about the parts that I didn't ~~read~~ – I mean – didn't understand while reading the (*Cliff Notes* version) book. This was a good book.

Since good vs. evil is the main theme of the book and since I also like good vs. evil comic books, like Batman vs. anybody, Superman vs. anybody, The Green Lantern vs. anybody, Wonder Woman vs. anybody, and even all the new movies that are remakes from *comic books*, I liked this story very much and told all my friends about how we ~~had to~~ read it in English class and although I didn't want to, I am glad I did because it was about good vs. evil.

For this timed test, I am supposed to write about good vs. evil in *Dr. Jekyll and Mr. Hyde*. You might guess from the title that one was good and one was evil. But which one? Just like me you will have to read the book (if you don't read the *Cliff Notes*,) to find out much more but I can share some things now.

Let me begin. Dr. Jekyll is a doctor and believes good and evil exists in everyone. That means you and me. I believe that to be true. We have our good side that we show everybody and our bad side that we don't. Ok. I guess I will have to tell you a bit about the story, although I really wanted to keep you guessing. Dr. Jekyll conducts experiments and something happens to him when he does. This is one reason you should read this book...to find out why. And then when you do, (will you tell me?) you will know.

We didn't see the movie because there wasn't a more modern version to "capture our interests" our teacher said. I wouldn't have minded watching a 1941 version so long as I learned something more about this story. I like movies that are made from books and I think I would have learned something new.

Dr. Jekyll walks with a cane and that has something to do with the plot. But you will have to find that out for yourself. And there are drugs involved, so maybe this book shouldn't be on the approved reading list in the first place. I mean, how did this book get approved anyway? Should we be reading about people taking drugs in the 19th century? I don't care if the drug was prescribed, that is a big deal these days for vulnerable teens to learn about in books. I might tell my parents about how I shouldn't have been made to read this book.

But my time is almost up as my teacher called out "ten minutes remaining" and grades are important to my parents, so I better keep writing because I don't think that idea of not reading this book well (at all) is going to work. This way just by turning in an essay, I might get a "50" instead of a zero grade on this assignment. Anything is better than a zero. Trust me. Anyway, something happens that is shocking, then something else happens that is more shocking, lots of letters are exchanged because this story is way before email, and then at the end the police get involved. I guess it is Scotland Yard because this book takes place in London, which I forgot to tell you earlier.

This is the kind of story that should be on ID Discovery TV. Then I'd be able to watch a screen version, which would help me a lot to understand all these twists and turns. Even with the (*Cliff*) notes we took in class, I got lost. I have wrestling practice every day and when I get home I didn't have time to read much. Every time I started reading I fell asleep. I really tried!

Our teacher says one more minute and our timed essay writing is up. So let me leave you with this:

"Who knows what evil lurks in the hearts of men? The Shadow knows." My favorite comic strip, which I read every day.

TIME!

Edgar Allan Poe's "The Black Cat" Timed Essay

"The Black Cat" is one of Edgar Allan Poe's most memorable short stories. The tale centers around a black cat and the subsequent deterioration of a man. The story is often linked with "The Tell-Tale Heart" because of the profound psychological elements these two works share. This first-person narrative falls into the realm of Horror/Gothic Literature and has been examined in association with themes of insanity and alcoholism.

Prompt: *What literary elements does Poe use to have the reader understand the deterioration of the storyteller as he tells his tale? Name the literary devices and give examples throughout the short story. For extra credit, you may describe someone you know who you have seen spiral out of control.*

Here, Kitty, Kitty
by
Claire D. Aisle

I am so excited you had us write about this topic. I, too, had a black cat, now deceased. My kitty was named Spooky, but we started calling him Boo. He roamed the neighborhood and never got in trouble, except once, when we couldn't find him for several days and worried that some wild creature in our neighborhood might have gobbled him up. My neighborhood was known to have sightings of a black bear, a cougar, definitely bobcats, foxes, and even an alligator. I'm not kidding! It was even in the paper about our menagerie of wild animals.

But in reality, Boo, was captured by a pre-teen who didn't have a cat and wanted to see what it was like to play around with one and Boo was so friendly, he did allow this ~~juvenile delinquent~~ young preteen to play with him and then that punk took him in his house, which he wasn't supposed to do because the family had dogs and Boo became really afraid and scampered away and hid under his parents' bed and he couldn't get him out and since he wasn't supposed to have another pet in the house anyway, much less one he captured against its will, he just ignored that the cat was in the house and especially under his parents' bed, and he didn't want to get in trouble, so he left it alone and then for two days when we couldn't find Boo, we were totally worried, but eventually he came home when finally the parents realized they had an scared animal under their bed and not knowing whose pet it was because they knew it was a pet, as Boo wore a collar, they let him outside and didn't know who to call about finding a cat under their bed and who might be worried their kitty hadn't been home in days, until one day they did find out it was us and eventually told us about the entire escapade two years later and they wondered as parents how our kitty got under their bed. Well, duh! Their ~~reform~~ middle school son was the culprit and they were the only ones who didn't know it and the reason we know it is because his older brother tattled on him one day and told us about his stupid little brother's behavior capturing our kitty because he saw it happen.

Anyway, I think this ~~moron~~ idiot brother might be a lot like the crazy narrator of the black cat he captured and tortured. See how real life imitates art? Or is it the other way around? Well, whatever that saying is. They are similar stories.

I do not know what ever happened to that little brother. He stayed inside a lot and only came out occasionally, like Halloween or other holidays where you could dress up and pretend you are something you are not. Like Mardi Gras. And then like sometimes Thanksgiving where one might dress up like a pilgrim. Certainly not St. Patrick's Day where he could be a leprechaun. Anyway, he didn't wear normal clothes and only came out when his parents were out of town, as in the case of our cat. He scooped our kitty up and took him home and then ignored him so he wouldn't get into trouble. Our Boo had nothing to eat or drink for two days. When he finally arrived home, he was so skinny, I knew something had scared him.

Poe's narrator was just as deranged as this kid in our neighborhood. I guess every neighborhood has one. Kinda like Boo Radley in *To Kill A Mockingbird* (see how I tied that in? His name was even Boo, too. I am thinking this is an extra-extra-credit moment!). Boo Radley only came out at night and watched people. We always brought our Boo in at night and especially Halloween as there are so many cruel people who might want to harm our black cat on that night.

Anyhow, crazy is as crazy does. And Poe is at his best writing about crazies.

Uh, oh, I see people are starting to put their pencils down so my time might be up. I want to add the literary elements so evident in the short story, but first let me say this...they say to write what you know and so...

TIME!

Edgar Allan Poe's "Annabel Lee" Timed Essay

My Favorite Cousin
by
Roger Overandoute

Prompt: *Decipher and retell this poem in prose, and in first person, after each stanza, as though this poem is your own. You have seventy-five minutes. Good luck!*

> It was many and many a year ago,
> In a kingdom by the sea,
> That a maiden there lived whom you may know
> By the name of Annabell Lee
> And this maiden she lived with no other thought
> Than to love and be loved by me.

When I was a child, my parents would take me to the beach. My younger cousin and I would build sandcastles in the sand by the shore. Her name was Annabel Lee and she was a very popular and well-liked little girl. We might spit and spat at times, she wanting the shovel when I had it or I might want her pail when she was using it to build our sandcastle, but we loved each other and generally got along well.

> I was a child and she was a child,
> In this kingdom by the sea;
> But we loved with a love that was more than love-
> I and my Annabel Lee;
> With a love that the winged seraphs of

heaven
Coveted her and me.

Again, we were really young children and I guess we must have built a lot of sandcastles, I don't remember, except that there must have been lots of different kinds of sandcastles we built because I mention it a lot. Personally, I think I would have rather built alligators, whales, or maybe a seahorse. Maybe even go hunting for shells, but obviously I stayed with my cousin and built sandcastles over and over with her.

> And this was the reason that, long ago,
> In this kingdom by the sea,
> A wind blew out of a cloud, chilling
> My beautiful Annabel Lee;
> So that her highborn kinsman came
> And bore her away from me,
> To shut her up in a sepulchre
> In this kingdom by the sea.

One day a wind blew through and she took a cold and my mother and her mother who are kin made her go inside because her nose started running and they didn't want her to catch a cold. But, too late! She did and died! I don't know what a sepulchre is, but I do know since my mother and her mother were sisters, they owned the beach property left to them by their father and so they buried her close by. I guess I built some more sandcastles in the sand around her grave, which is a very odd thing to do.

> The angels, not half so happy in heaven,
> Went envying her and me-

Yes!- that was the reason (as all men know,
In this kingdom by the sea)
That the wind came out of the cloud by night,
Chilling and killing my **Annabel Lee**.

I already explained this in the stanza above. Geez, why all the redundancy? It's like those people who tell a story and then retell a second time as though you didn't get it the first time around. I hear 'ya. Trust me, I get it.

But our love it was stronger by far than the love
Of those who were older than we-
Of many far wiser than we-
And neither the angels in heaven above,
Nor the demons down under the sea,
Can ever dissever my soul from the soul
Of the beautiful Annabel Lee.

Ok, now, this really gets creepier. We were first cousins, for heaven's sake! And we were children. What did we know about love in the adult sense? Are we supposed to be reading stuff like this in English class? And our souls are still attached? I just knew her that summer at the beach. I haven't really thought about her since. We were around five. I don't even remember what she looks like. She's dead. I've moved on. My mother and Annabel Lee's mother, who is my aunt, had a fight after that beach trip and they didn't talk for two years, although they lived in the same town. Mama told me it had something to do with the pictures we took on the seashore – well, it was really a beach – and one of them wanted to keep a certain picture and not share it so they had a big brouhaha about it. I don't know more than that, but believe me, I haven't thought about my cousin much.

> For the moon never beams without
> bringing me dreams
> Of the beautiful Annabel Lee;
> And the stars never rise but I feel the
> bright eyes
> Of the beautiful Annabel Lee;
> And so, all the night-tide, I lie down by
> the side
> Of my darling- my darling- my life and
> my bride,
> In the sepulchre there by the sea,
> In her tomb by the sounding sea.

Thank goodness I am at the end. I've already said I don't think much about my cousin except at night in my dreams when there is a full moon and stars. Yeah, right. Annabel Lee beautiful? She was OK cute, as I remember but beautiful? Oh, no, here is a really gross part. This poem should be told on "American Horror Story" during the week of Halloween. Did my parents hatch up some kind of marriage plan with my cousin? They are sick! And I am not going to go lie down by her grave where I built all those stupid sandcastles making it a sand kingdom. No sirree. To tell you the truth, I bet the tides have washed those sandcastles away, too.

This is just a gross poem. I am just going to quit now even before my time runs out.

"The Legend of Sleepy Hollow" Timed Essay

"The Legend of Sleepy Hollow" is a gothic story by American author Washington Irving and is among the earliest examples of American fiction with enduring popularity, especially during Halloween because of a character known as the Headless Horseman believed to be a Hessian soldier who was decapitated by a cannonball in battle. Allusion is a brief and indirect reference to a person, place, thing, or idea of historical, cultural, literary, or political significance. It does not describe in detail the person or thing to which it refers. It is just a passing comment and the writer expects the reader to possess enough knowledge to spot the allusion and grasp its importance in a text. You have 65 minutes to identify and support three allusions in "The Legend of Sleepy Hollow".

Heads Will Roll
by
Ali Moe

When I was in elementary school, I first heard of this story. Disney even created a mini video version which we watched in school. In the small 1790s town of Sleepy Hollow near New York, a gangly schoolteacher, Ichabod Crane, comes to town. He is so much like my friend, who shall not be named here because she goes to this school: she looks like him, she does not realize that she captivates all the boys in school, and she is superstitious like the schoolteacher.

Like Crane, (and let me add here her last name is Bird – please do not tell the other teachers but I thought it more than coincidental and I was hoping for extra credit) since she is tall, thin, and although my good friend, just down right unattractive. Bless her heart. She really looks like the female version of Crane from the Disney movie – pointed hook nose, dry dark hair parted down the middle, big ears, toothy grin, and that stupid ponytail that they both wear. And my childhood heartthrob, Juan Morefore DeRhode, can't stop looking and flirting with her! Do people tend to emulate their names? Bird? Crane? I remember watching "Frasier" reruns on television and Dr. Frasier Crane had a big cranium and they poked fun at him because of it. There was an episode about his getting a caricature that would be hung in a very popular Seattle restaurant that showcased his huge forehead and he was vain enough to not want it displayed.

And my middle school boyfriend, Dawson D. Towel, thinks she is the cat's meow. She is like catnip to all the boys in high school, and he is still just as bewitched (more extra credit?) by her like all the other high school boys now. She and Ichabod could both charm the skin off a snake.

But I think their biggest comparison is that they are both superstitious. Brom Bones, the local rough and tough guy, is irked by Crane's popularity with the women and a subtle rivalry erupts. Since Brom knows about this teacher's weakness, he plays it to his advantage by telling him the legend of the fearsome Headless Horseman to frighten the teacher. After a party at Katrina Van Tassel's home who both suitors are sweet on, Crane's lonely night ride home becomes more lively than he ever imagined as the Horseman appears to chase him and almost scares the pants off Ichabod.

I, too, played a trick on my girlfriend, who my ex-boyfriend, Tab Collar, started seeing after we broke up (not my choice). My girlfriend, Robin Bird, once had to have cataract surgery and while her parents were at work and were only able to take her *to* her appointment, I promised them I would pick her up *from* the appointment and bring her home. Cataract surgery? Yes, Robin wore thick glasses (another reason to find her unattractive) at an early age because of her bad eyesight, but being the good friend that I am, I offered to take her home after her outpatient surgery.

She was feeling fine except for her eyes being bandaged, and I suggested we get ice cream after her surgery, because doesn't ice cream make everything better? It did after my tonsils were taken out. I told her I'd park close to the ice cream shop and gently lead her from the car to the ice cream parlor. I knew they were working on a second story window on the sidewalk near the ice cream parlor and they had placed a ladder there in front of that location, so I carefully lead her down the sidewalk and under the ladder. This superstitious girl had no idea!

It must have been my day for revenge because just as we passed under the ladder, a black cat darted in front of us.

Our teacher got up from her desk after looking at her iPhone so it must mean it's about time to end all this.

And one of the best "Don't get mad, get even" lines from the movie, *Animal House*, was that she could only schedule her outpatient surgery on a Friday. And that month it was Friday, the 13th. Double Whammy! She was aware of the date, so that's why I suggested ice cream - to comfort her.

When I told her all her indiscretions about walking under a ladder, appointment on Friday the 13th, a black cat crossed in front of her, she didn't take it well. How was all that my fault? I did the best I could to look after her while she was bandaged up.

My friend and Ichabod Crane have so much in common. Oh, wait. I wasn't supposed to mention comparisons? We had to write about allusions? I thought it means what the story alluded to? Oh, gosh, I have really screwed up. Well, let's see if I still have enough time to mention…NO!

TIME!

The Revolutionary War Timed Essay

Quote from Shakespeare's *Twelfth Night*: "Some are born great, some achieve greatness, and some have greatness thrust upon 'em." (Act II, Scene v). Describe the iconic patriot, Samuel Adams, using this quote.

Samuel Adams
-Such an Iconic Patriot, They Named a Beer After Him
by
Ben D. Rules

Although my American History teacher is my favorite teacher in high school, I tend to also learn a lot from the comedy television show, *Drunk History*. Although inebriated, the narrator provides good information about a person or event in history.

Last week they featured Sam Adams. To me, it looks like he had mother issues for several reasons: a) even after attending college, he did not find the kind of work that interested him as a young man, so he moved home and became an adult dependent living off his parents and their money and b) moving back home to live with his mother and father, did he misplace his feelings for his mother when he couldn't cut the umbilical cord at home but was obsessed with doing so against his *mother* country?

He was a rabble-rouser!

Furious, he harnessed popular resentment against Parliament's authority to tax colonies. Why was he so upset? It wasn't *his* money. But one day, I guess it would be. Maybe this was another resentment towards his *mother,* as she would inherit their wealth should his father pass on first. And his family was pretty well off selling malts to beer breweries. Is this where he found his love of beer? Although a devout Puritan, he still frequented a lot the taverns in Boston. He didn't care what was thought about his affection for beer unlike the Boston Baptist Puritans. Oh, those Baptist Puritans still drank, they just didn't drink in downtown Boston. They traveled to the next town to purchase and consume theirs. They thought other Baptists wouldn't notice when they took their swigs. But there were other Baptist Puritans from Boston doing the exact same thing! Just like the Baptists of today. They go to the next town over to purchase their liquor so they will not be seen since they drink and don't want anyone to notice. Is this an inherited trait?

Although Sam Adams may have been a drunk, at least he wasn't a hypocrite. Or he might say he was selling his homegrown malts to the local breweries, so *that's why* he was in the taverns a lot. But guess what? His father did pass first. Sam's mother (not knowing his ill will against her) let him take over the malt business and he proves my point. He ran it into the ground.

And that's why I don't see how that Frederick Shakespeare quote relates to Sam. So I am not going to try to defend one of those arguments. He certainly didn't measure up to those three choices. Generally on our multiple choice tests, there is a fourth choice, like 'd) none of the above.' Why didn't you have one of those? Although you are my favorite teacher, not having a fourth choice, like we are all use to, is lame. I mean, you prepare us for standardized testing with four choices. How can we expect less? I feel cheated. If I had a fourth choice, I might choose it and then could finish this essay with another idea.

Clock says I have fifteen minutes but I can always count on Vic Trola. He has to take shots every hour on the hour, so he is sent to the office to have someone administer it. I don't know what it's for and even during our timed tests, he has to leave to get his shots. So, since he has been once already, that means that at least one hour is already up and our essay time should end soon. They didn't announce for him to come to the office this time like they usually do over the intercom in every class I have with him when they say, ""Would Vic Trola please report to the office?" and I guess because we are taking a quiet timed test, so this time they just let him go out of the room to get his shots without the announcement, "Would Vic Trola please report to the office?" The school nurse helps him or something. Lucky Duck. He gets out of class a lot. I wish I did. Maybe I could fake something to get me out of class like I have a jellybean stuck up my nose or something.

Anyway, as it is, the three choices threw me off. Why couldn't Edward Shakespeare not have a fourth choice? Was he too lazy to think of another?

Personally, I think Sam Adams might have been depressed and just loved to hear himself talk. Rebellious by nature and enjoying the *malts of his labor* – hope you get that reference- he established The Sons of Liberty. I am sure they sat around drinking beer from their pewter tankards and pontificating (two big words – hope I get extra credit) their thoughts. I like seeing those pewter mugs with beer in them. *Not for me, of course.*

I bet Sam and Paul Revere had some good times enjoying their taverns' beers and discussing the war. I would like to have been a fly on the wall overhearing one of their conversations about what Paul was going to be involved in like…

TIME!

The American Revolution Timed Essay

Prompt: Benjamin Franklin wore many hats: indentured apprentice; printer, publisher and postmaster; scientist and inventor; politician and booster; diplomat; and ladies' man. Pick one and by using examples from our reading, describe Ben Franklin during that period of his life. You have seventy-five minutes.

He Ain't Heavy; He's My Brother
By
Poppy Flowers

I chose Benjamin Franklin from his early years living in Boston. He was introduced to printing and journalism by his brother, James, and started working with him as an apprentice when he was twelve. But he was an indentured worker! He could not earn money and therefore was bound to James until he turned twenty-one. I can see where I might be sick of my brother by then, too, and run away to Philadelphia, which is what Ben did.

I don't have a brother, but I have a twin sister and there is no getting away from her. And worse, our parents thought they were so clever giving us flora names both beginning in "P". They dressed us alike even up into middle school and we hated it. Once when my sister wasn't feeling well and stayed home, I was walking down the hall of my middle school and suddenly a teacher who I didn't know and hadn't seen before, pulled me aside and started yelling at me saying, "How dare you walk by my room after you skipped class!" I doubted she would go for my excuse about a twin sister. I had to get a teacher I knew to tell her that I was a twin.

It is interesting though, that although not twins, the Franklin brothers had the same interests. Even though my sister and I have different interests, we do have the same sneaky and playful behavior. After that innocent middle school incident, we decided to band together and pull some tricks on people. Last year my sister was dating a guy from another school. When he came to our house to pick her up for a date, I opened the door. He told me he liked my new hairstyle and kissed me. I invited him inside and then yelled up the stairs, "Your boyfriend is here." You should have seen the look on his face.

Another time we both worked at the Wendy's drive-thru. We shared the same car so we asked for the same shift and rode together to work. The manager was young and wanted to mess with people so he would put my sister at the pay window and me at the food window just to see their reaction. That was brilliant.

I will say that rascally behavior did bring us closer. But I don't remember our teacher telling us that the Franklin brothers were very close especially after Ben played a trick on his older brother, James. When he was sixteen, he wanted to write for his brother's newspaper but James was something of a bully and wouldn't allow it. So, Ben snuck around and made up the name Silence Dogood whose witty and satirical letters covered a range of topics from courtship to education. Our teacher told us he would leave these letters on the newspaper's front doorstep and his brother thought they were good enough to be printed never knowing the source.

Fifteen of his letters were published, resulting in the amusement of the newspaper's readers. The pretend Mrs. Dogood received several marriage proposals and this resulted in brother James' ire.

There are students standing at the classroom door wanting to get in, so my time must almost be up.

Quickly, since we are on the subject of siblings, did you ever hear about the prank my sister and I pulled last year? She was president of the Junior class and I was Vice-President. When it was re-election time and we had to give our speeches for this year (our Senior year), she completely forgot about staying after school to give hers and walked home. I remembered and gave my speech for Vice-President. A girlfriend of mine stayed after school with me, swapped t-shirts with me, and watched me walk up to give the presidential speech on the spot for my sister. Wasn't sure it would work, but as you know, we both won.

Don't tell anybody, please. Let's keep it our secret since we only have two more weeks until graduation.

To think Ben Franklin played pranks for sport in the 1730s just like my sister and I do today. I took French for three years but my sister took three years of Spanish. If I ever go down the Language Arts hall and her Spanish teacher is standing out for hall duty, she'll stop me and start spitting out Spanish words that I don't know expecting me to communicate with her in Spanish so one time I...

TIME!

Paul Revere - An American Revolutionary Hero
Timed Essay

You learned from class the true purpose of Paul
Revere during the Revolutionary War: to race to
Concord to warn Patriots Samuel Adams and John
Hancock that British troops - 700 of them - were
marching to Concord to arrest them.
Prompt: Why were Paul Revere's efforts so
memorable to the cause of revolution and separating
from England?

Paul Revere – The Midnight Rider
by
Willie Maikett

Well, I've got to run to keep from hiding
And I'm bound to keep on riding
And I've got one more silver dollar
But I'm not gonna let them catch me, no
Not gonna let 'em catch the midnight rider…
~The Allman Brothers

I have always loved The Allman Brothers although
they are a band from my grandparents' generation. I
think the words from "The Midnight Rider" fit
perfectly for the title of this essay. Paul Revere had
much in common with these lyrics…He was a
silversmith, he was running ahead of the British
Army, and he rode at midnight, or so the story goes.
In reality he did help organize an intelligence and
alarm system to keep watch on the British military.
    Paul Revere's lonesome ride at midnight to warn
the colonies that the "British were coming" is
something that every American student learns in

grade school. But there's a problem. This story isn't entirely accurate. Historical stories change over time and in this case, people think of Paul Revere as the lone rider bringing the news of the British invasion because of the poem by Henry Wadsworth Longfellow in 1860. So, what really happened and how is it different from what we thought?

This is how I think it went down: On April 18, 1775, it is true that Paul Revere did participate in a system alerting some members of the Sons of Liberty that British troops had been seen gathering to attack military stores in Concord, Massachusetts. Once *he* was warned of the impending launch of British troops, the lantern story of "one if by land and two if by sea" was the signal for the militia.

But how was Revere warned? We don't often hear that story. If Revere was an organizer of this new intelligence system, wouldn't…wait a minute, my shoe needs tying.

It's been twenty minutes because as I was tying my shoe and getting settled back in my seat, I came up too fast and bumped my head on the corner of my desk and it started bleeding. My teacher saw this and the entire class turned and looked at me and now she has to write up the fact that there was a distraction in the classroom while we were taking our assessment essay and I can't help that. But my name is going on some list and I may be in hot water and I sure hope we don't have to retake the entire exam because of my clumsiness.

And I sure hope this incident doesn't go on my permanent record because I need to attend a good college, so I can get a good job as an aerospace engineer like my dad because if I don't he'll be disappointed in me and I can't stand when I have let him down, which it seems like I do a lot.

Not my brother, though. He's the really smart one. He is at MIT and is on the Dean's List and everything. I am lucky to just tread water. And here I have gone and hit my head and we may have to start this stupid test all over another time because I caused a distraction and according the rules our teacher read to us before we started writing, if anything "is amiss", she has to report it. Stuff like this always happens to me.

Uh, oh…she's heading this way…I'm doomed. Somebody call…

TIME!

Daughters of The American Revolution College Scholarship and Grants

Essay Application
for
The Daughters of the American Revolution College Scholarship and Grants

Criteria Used on College Scholarships and Grants for High School Students
Many students often have questions about what panels and committees look for when selecting scholarship recipients. Overall, scholarships can be based on a variety of different factors including academic achievement, test scores, community involvement, <u>written essays</u>, volunteerism, etc. While students who have high GPAs and solid test scores will often qualify for many scholarship opportunities, it should be understood that even if you do not have a perfect 4.0 GPA you may still be eligible for a variety of scholarships based on other factors. Toward that end, be sure to take advantage of the opportunity to become involved in volunteer and community service activities.

Dear Daughters of the American Revolution Scholarship/Grant Committee,

When my counselor told me about this possible scholarship, I jumped at the chance to apply and send in my written essay. Besides my GPA, academic achievement, test scores, community involvement, volunteerism, etc. I should write about my desire to become a chick sexer.

It may surprise you to know that my parents, and grandparents, and great-grandparents farmed. It is a very reputable and respectable job. I played and worked on their farms since I could walk. We had many types of animals on our farm, except goats because every pound of tin cans swallowed turned into five pounds of slimy fecal pellets. But no one ever tells you that.

In the movies you see beautiful barns with hay, but the truth is the hay in the barns is especially gross, especially if you have cows. A cow only digests two percent of what they eat. So where does the rest go? It spews out in waste. I mean, the life cycle of a cow is ruining grass, or hay, and death. So the hay, or even grass, is filled with feces and you think, hey, I cleaned it up with a shovel. But nope, they are peeing on that hay or grass as well. And when you go to try to move the fecal matter with urine on top, ammonia shoots out to burn your lungs and sear your eyeballs.

That's why I want to become a chick sexer. You may not know what that is but a chick sexer is someone who determines the sex of chickens. You may think that is hard, but once you have been trained to know what to look for, it's easy as pie. I am well qualified as I have been in 4-H ever since elementary school. Well, really since fifth grade. But because I live and worked on a farm, I was voted four out of six times, *Farmer of the Year* in 4-H. If Bud Vase hadn't gotten sick with some rare disease in seventh and eighth grade before he died, I would have won that award those two years. He was a nice guy and all. Just sayin'.

I must also mention, that I would babysit chickens for my neighboring farmers when their families took mini-vacations, I was President of the Stop-Chick-Fil-A From Building a Drive-Thru on Hall Street, Vice-President of the Eat More Beef Club at my high school, and judge at Pick the Prettiest Chick Contest at our county fair the last four years. I never entered one of my beautiful chickens because of the nepotism mentality of the contest. It was bad enough that my three cousins on my mother's side of the family entered their chickens in the contest, my dad's sister's children entered theirs, and my own sister brought one from our farm. Judging that contest was tough and it also brought threats to my life…that's how important it was for them to win.

I would be honored to represent the Daughters of the Russian (or American?)Revolution as your chosen student. I would make you proud and I sure could use the money. My Uncle Mo, my dad's older brother and first son of the family, inherited what little money there was when my granddaddy died. Granny had already passed and Uncle Mo, being the firstborn son, took the money and buried it somewhere on his daddy's property. However, he is a drunk and he can't remember where, although we have been trying to find it for almost two years now.

Chickens are my life. I think being a chick sexer is a very important job to know who's doing what to whom and how many chickadees you can expect in any given season. If you can't count the sexes, how would you know what kind of crop you are going to yield?

Kansas Agriculture College is starting a new program this coming year for a degree in chick sexing. I would love to be in their first graduating class.

Thank you for your consideration. And please don't eat at Chick-Fil-A, Kentucky Fried Chicken, Bojangles, Dairy Queen, Popeye's, McDonald's, Wendy's, Burger King, Zaxby's, or any other restaurant that serves fried chicken. I know you have heard of the saying, "Running around like a chicken with his head cut off," well, that's because chickens have feelings, too.

Sincerely,
Rufus Leaking

Essay Application
for
The Daughters of the American Revolution College
Scholarship and Grants

Criteria Used on College Scholarships and Grants
for High School Students
Many students often have questions about what
panels and committees look for when selecting
scholarship recipients. Overall, scholarships can be
based on a variety of different factors including
academic achievement, test scores, community
involvement, written essays, volunteerism, etc. While
students who have high GPAs and solid test scores
will often qualify for many scholarship opportunities,
it should be understood that even if you do not have a
perfect 4.0 GPA you may still be eligible for a variety
of scholarships based on other factors. Toward that
end, be sure to take advantage of the opportunity to
become involved in volunteer and community service
activities.

Dear Daughters of the American Revolution
Scholarship/Grant Committee,

Thank you so much for sponsoring scholarships or
grants for high school students. My great-aunt, that is
my mama's aunt, encouraged me to inform you of my
hopes and dreams after high school. My great-aunt
Gracie told me that her stepsister had once been in
your organization. I am hoping that this stepsister, no
intimate relation to my side of the family, might still
give me a leg up on qualifying by some sort of
almost-a-DAR-member-by-a-blended-marriage-but-
no-actual-DNA. Perhaps that's just wishful thinking!

Anyhow, because of my unique skills as a hair boiler down at the town plant, I thought maybe you might be looking for someone needing a scholarship other than your typical doctors, lawyers, teachers, and such. It pays really good money, I am told. More than teachers, I hear, so I have ambition!

What is a hair boiler you ask? It is someone who boils animal hair until it curls and is used in a variety of products, which I signed a contract saying I could not talk about it anymore than that. Besides, you wouldn't want to know. Promise. I will say you'd be grossed out if you knew all the animal hair that was boiled and used in your home.

And the pay that I mentioned? I know men down at the plant making $150,000. I just need to have a college education to become a manager someday. Thought I'd start now. I have ambition!

Please consider me as you now see how different this ambition is and yet how necessary, we need hair boilers.

Thank you,
Baxter Nature

Essay Application
For
The Daughters of the American Revolution College
Scholarship and Grants

Criteria Used on College Scholarships and Grants
for High School Students
Many students often have questions about what
panels and committees look for when selecting
scholarship recipients. Overall, scholarships can be
based on a variety of different factors including
academic achievement, test scores, community
involvement, written essays, volunteerism, etc. While
students who have high GPAs and solid test scores
will often qualify for many scholarship opportunities,
it should be understood that even if you do not have a
perfect 4.0 GPA you may still be eligible for a variety
of scholarships based on other factors. Toward that
end, be sure to take advantage of the opportunity to
become involved in volunteer and community service
activities.

Dear Daughters of the American Revolution
Scholarship/Grant Committee,

I am very excited for this opportunity to apply for
your scholarship or grant given to students who
decide on interesting career paths and need monetary
help. It will fulfill a desire to improve where I work
now with the help of training and education, should I
receive an offer.

Currently I work at the Standing Room Only
movie theater on Skate-or-Bowl Road, next to the
Skate-or-Bowl Complex. I am sure you have been
there to see afternoon movies at our reduced price.

Why would someone of your age pay full price? And also why would you go at night when you have to drive home, possibly alone, and find yourself walking into an empty, dark house? The afternoon prices are the best, don't you think? Especially if you are a Senior Citizen like I am sure most of you are.

My current job is working behind the food counter. I get to be with food and customers all day and I love it! But I'd like to get ahead and become something more. No, not selling tickets behind the glass booth, nor greeter pointing people to their movie theater destination, not even a theater manager. My chosen field is something you'd see every time you might take in a movie at Standing Room Only or any other movie theater. And I bet you hadn't even thought about it at all.

My dream job is to be a Cheese Sprayer!

What is a Cheese Sprayer, you ask? It's a person who sprays cheese or butter by hand on popcorn. And since it is by hand, it takes skill. Our local community college is offering a certificate for this chosen profession. But it costs money that I don't have.

I just love popcorn, don't you? You've seen those big bags at your local grocery store on the end caps of an aisle. The popcorn comes in two flavors: buttered and cheese. It just never occurred to you, did it, that a specially, skilled artisan is behind all that flavor!

I am sure, now, you appreciate what goes behind that delicious popcorn flavor you like either in the movie theater or your own local grocery store. It takes a specially certified popcorn technician to carefully spray that great flavor evenly on each piece. And I am just the gal to do it.

Should I receive the scholarship or grant, come by the theater sometime during the day when it's less crowded and should you see me behind the counter, please introduce yourself and I'll sneak you a small bag of popcorn and you can even choose your flavor!

In advance, thank you for any help you might bestow.

Sincerely,
Barbie Kew

The School Myth Exposed – One Student's Case Study Personal Records for Kenny Maikett

You know the saying. "This is going on your permanent record."

Yikes! Can the less-than-desirable things you've done throughout your academic career be complied in one location and that this permanent record is something that could end up in anyone's hands and detrimentally affect your future? That's a scary thought.

But are they real or a myth? According to the U.S. Department of Education, there are real education records for each student, so it is not a myth. However, this 'permanent record' is actually just record keeping on all students who are currently attending, or have attended, a public, parochial, or private school. This record is just a form filled out by parents at the beginning of each school year, which obtains personal identifying information for their student, such as name, address, phone number, parents' names, and contact information.

Commonly it also records details such as class grades, important test scores, attendance records, health and immunization information, discipline records, special awards conferred, previous schools attended, etc. In other words – it is nothing to be frightened about. It's just a log of various information that is unique to each student.

Student records do not exist solely to keep track of all the terrible (or not so terrible) behaviors one had exhibited during your school years. They may be present, but those things are by no means the reason for its existence.

But I recently was able to get ahold of the private school records of Kenny Maikett from Bunkum, Maine, so I guess there are exceptions. Here are his instructors' yearly pupil growth surveys beginning in 1952.

Grade: 1
General Academic Appraisal: B-
Overall Citizenship Evaluation: B+
Times Tardy: 0
Fidgeting or Talking Out of Turn: Occasionally
Comments: Kenny Maikett picks his nose and eats what he finds.

Grade: 2
General Academic Appraisal: B-
Overall Citizenship Evaluation: B+
Times Tardy: 0
Days Absent: 3 (no excuse note sent to office)
Fidgeting or Talking out of Turn: Occasionally
Comments: He still continues to pick his nose but I have not seen him eat anything he finds. An improvement over last year. Parents must have discouraged such behavior. Now eats dried glue.

Grade: 3
General Academic Appraisal: B-
Overall Citizenship Evaluation: B+
Times Tardy: 3 (no note as to why he was tardy)
Days Absent: 3 (excuse note from parents sent to office – dental appointments {so they say})
Fidgeting or Talking Out of Turn: Occasionally

Comments: Kenny is mesmerized with pretending he has guns while playing on the playground during recess. He says he is the Lone Ranger and uses his pretend gun(s) to arrest other school children for various reasons like those wearing white socks, which means he arrests everyone – boys and girls – because they only wear white socks. He tries to put them in a 'holding section' of the playground under the slide, but the children who do go under the slide, leave on their own free will and Kenny cannot maintain doing both – arresting and watching over the cell mates, which totally frustrates him and he starts kicking rocks.

Grade: 4
General Academic Appraisal: C+
Overall Citizenship Evaluation: B-
Times Tardy: 2 (note from parents why he was tardy – at dentist for dental work {they said})
Days Absent: 0
Fidgeting or Talking out of Turn: No, but he slumps in his desk a lot.
Comments: Kenny does not keep a tidy desk. May not be college material.

Junior High School Grades 6-8

Grade: 6
General Academic Appraisal: B-
Overall Citizenship Evaluation: B-
Times Tardy: 0

Days Absent: <u>5 1/2 (Rhinoplasty surgery – but should have done something about his teeth before now as he will be picked on no matter how good his nose looks).</u>
Fidgeting or Talking out of Turn: <u>Twiddles his forefinger and thumb through his hair constantly.</u>
Comments: <u>Keeps a comic book inside his academic book to read and thinks his teachers do not notice. They do and after several attempts he was made to stay after school.</u>

Grade: <u>7</u>
General Academic Appraisal: <u>C+</u>
Overall Citizenship Evaluation: <u>B-</u>
Times Tardy: <u>1</u>
Fidgeting or Talking out of Turn: <u>Constantly</u>
Comments: <u>Gym coaches noticed he looks at other boys for a length of time while dressing out for class. They said, "Longer than he should."</u>

Grade: <u>8</u>
General Academic Appraisal: <u>C</u>
Overall Citizenship Evaluation: <u>D+</u>
Times Tardy: <u>2</u>
Fidgeting or Talking out of Turn: <u>Kenny has warmed every seat in the classroom at some time or another. There is no place to put him where he doesn't talk.</u>
Comments: <u>He cleans out his ears with his pencil and not with the eraser end. That's just gross.</u>

Personal Records for Kenny Maikett
High School
9th – 12th grades

Grade: <u>9</u>

General Academic Appraisal: <u>C-</u>
Overall Citizenship Evaluation: <u>C</u>
Times Tardy: <u>3</u>
Fidgeting or Talking out of Turn: <u>Fidgets with his pants zipper.</u>
Comments: <u>Sitting alphabetically in classes, he sits two desks ahead of Emmy Nems and continues to intentionally drop his pencil, and while picking it up he turns around, and tries to look up her dress when doing so.</u>

Grade: <u>10</u>
General Academic Appraisal: <u>C-</u>
Overall Citizenship Evaluation: <u>D+</u>
Times Tardy: <u>4</u>
Fidgeting or Talking out of Turn: <u>Always</u>
Comments: <u>Fails to shower after Physical Education.</u>

Grade: <u>11</u>
General Academic Appraisal: <u>C-</u>
Overall Citizenship Evaluation: <u>D</u>
Times Tardy: <u>5</u>
Fidgeting or Talking out of Turn: <u>Loud and high voice, nervous laughter. Sounds like a girl.</u>
Comments: <u>At last parent teacher conference, father wore brown shoes with a blue suit. He wore the same suit and shoes at PTA meeting in September, October, and January. There was no December PTA meeting.</u>

Grade: <u>12</u>
General Academic Appraisal: <u>C+</u>
Overall Citizenship Evaluation: <u>D-</u>
Times Tardy: <u>5</u>
Fidgeting or Talking out of Turn: <u>Fidgets with his pants zipper.</u>

Comments: Must not have learned anything in Health or Physical Education class because of his misuse of proper words associated with and identifying the human body both male and female. Overheard by teachers among his peers. Teachers discussing holding his diploma until he retakes those classes.

Sample writing Senior Year:
Prompt: What is your opinion of the education you received and after graduation, what are your plans for your immediate future and beyond? Please do not exceed 250 words.

After graduation, I have plans for my immediate future and beyond. My favorite subject is math and I hope to attend college and major in the math and science fields like outer space. Being an astronaut may be out of the question as I am not tall enough at the moment, and I am not good looking enough with all my dandruff, acne pimples, halitosis, athlete's foot, blackhead pores, and bad posture. I may have to work behind the scenes as an engineer. I do perspire a lot and I hope that won't interfere with my studies and future jobs. I wear glasses and I notice a lot of engineers do, too.
I have a good work ethic. You can ask Mrs. Holly Cost. Every summer from 10th -12th grades, I have worked for her mowing lawns and always showed up on time to do my job unless it rained or my mom couldn't wake me up after someone had a party at their house the night before. During the Fall and Winter, I was a dishwasher and later promoted to busboy at Shoney's Big Boy Restaurant. One night they let me work the cash register because of my math skills. But when patrons complained about

having to view my acne just after having eaten their meal, I was then demoted back to busboy.
I could write more but I am at 249 words and will keep it under the requirement. But honestly? I think high school sucked.

Teacher notes: Student still has acne and may not be able hold down a face-to-face job in the near future. He is probably correct to be "behind the scenes" in whatever profession he chooses as he is an average child. His eyesight should be evaluated again because even with his thick glasses, he still squints. He is a nice boy, but do not get too close because of his body odor. He seemed to like high school while attending. I think he must have good math skills as he counted the number of words correctly at 249 and stopped writing to follow the writing instruction.

Psychological Profile by school psychologist, Dr. Chad A. While.

Bunkum High School's Faculty and Student Obituaries

Anna Maria Alberghetti Cuomo

Anna Maria Alberghetti Cuomo, age 72, passed away in Bunkum, Maine Thanksgiving Eve. She leaves behind a possible husband (not sure) and her Bull Nose Terrier, Bingo. If her name sounds familiar it is because she was named for her parents' favorite actress and child prodigy.

Before moving to Bunkum for her father's employment in the bakery business, the Cuomos lived in New York. They heard Anna Maria sing at Carnegie Hall when she was 13. At fifteen, she was introduced to American film audiences acting alongside Bing Crosby, Red Skelton, among others. So mesmerized by her beauty and talent, when their only daughter was born, they named her after the actress, singer, and Tony-Award winner hoping she too, might live up to that famous talent.

But, alas, she did not. Anna Maria Alberghetti Cuomo was the complete opposite. She was the last child in her family of six boys and developed her rough and tough persona because of their influence. Anna Maria was an acnephilia – a person who derives pleasure from popping pimples or zits on either one's own face or someone close to them. When her brothers went through puberty and Anna Maria was just a mere child, to get their attention, she loved to pop their acne pimples. Because she had no qualms of popping theirs or anyone else's pimples, she inherited several nicknames. The ones that her brothers called her was ZITzie but her friends at school Ditzie Zitzie because she did not make good grades while at Bunkum High School. She is remembered for homesteading the girls' lavatory, popping friends' back pimples between classes, especially Patty Cakes, who had the largest pimple ever seen by the girls at Bunkum High. Her zit was located under her armpit. She called it her third boob until Anna Maria solved her problem for her. If ever there were squeals coming from the girls' restroom, it was sure to involve Anna Maria and her zit-popping activities.

She was also remembered for having an altercation with Linda Hahnd in Girls' Restroom - Hall 3, when she told Linda, "Watch it, skank. You-ah knock-ah my mascara brush inna sink again and I'll rip every hair outta ya head!"

Anna Maria wore black net stockings all her life, never changed her ratted sky-high bee-hive hairdo from her 1964 Senior Class picture, wore three-inch nails with various nail colors depending on the season, smacked gum all her life, and kept in shape by continuing her roller skating from a young age at the Skate-or-Bowl Roller Rink and Bowling Alley up until her passing last month. The fact the skating and bowling rink stayed in business that long is an accomplishment in and of itself. She didn't just skate on Geriatric Night. She skated with every age group and could be heard swearing to the toddlers, "Getta outta my way, you punk. You're takin' up the flippin' floor space. Yeah, keep 'ya crying to yourself or better yet, go blab to your mudda."

Anna Maria was in the Future Cosmetologist Club her Junior and Senior years. She later attended Cut and Caboodle College to obtain her hairdresser and cosmetologist certificates. She remained a popular,

although trash mouthy, hairdresser at Hair to Please
You, until her death.

Obituary for Miss Flora Ann Fauna

We once heard this happened but it was not true. But with a terrible turn of events, today we find out it really is and friends and family are sad to learn of the passing of Flora Ann Fauna due to a tragic greenhouse accident last week in her backyard.

Flora Ann was once thought to have died thirty years ago in her hometown of Bunkum, Maine. She was supposedly involved in a kiln accident while making a pot for display at the Bunkum Visual Arts Center for the Blind. Her pot was to be seen, bid on to raise money for the center, and then sold to the highest bidder. But this turned out to be a false rumor. Flora Ann was very much alive until last week.

Flora Ann Fauna died from her injuries after falling off her ladder while trying to adjust the overhead fan in her hothouse for her plants. An award winning orchid grower, she was ahead of the craze of supplying black orchids to girls around the country for prom and other formal dances.

Flora Ann graduated in 1964 from Bunkum High School. Her senior picture describes her as "She marches to a different drummer." As a free spirit, she was ahead of the times or behind the times, as she was a fan of not only Joan Baez but also she collected Burl Ives' records. She ironed her hair at a time when most girls in 1964 were ratting theirs. She did not understand the "Bigger the Hair, the Closer to Heaven" or sometimes called, "Tease It for Jesus" mentality. While her peers at BHS were wearing plaid skirts with socks and saddle-oxfords, she was wearing tights under her skirts with ballet slippers.

She was a member of the future Freedom Riders. She participated in the Senior Class Play, *Julius*

Caesar, as assistant to the assistant stage manager. She played her guitar and sang, "Michael Rowed the Boat Ashore, Alleluia" and an encore performance of "Hang Down Your Head, Tom Dooley", in the annual Senior Stunt Night.

She was member of the Hootenanny Club, 4; Leaf & Squib, 1,2,3,4; Drama Club, 1,2,3,4; Guitar Club, 4; Clay Pot Society, 3,4.

Also known as artsy-craftsy-spooky-kooky she landed a "scholarship" from Art Instruction, Inc., a correspondence art school she saw in the back of her mother's *Good Housekeeping Magazine*. She was recognized for her initial talent by drawing the head of a Santa 5" high and in pencil. After sending off her drawing, to this home study art school, or "college" as she chose to tell people, she had high hopes of earning the $150/week it professed it's students could earn as commercial artists.

The winner of these drawing contests from the magazine ads also offered "free" art course training (with the freedom of studying at home) AND art textbooks and supplies. For years, Flora Ann attempted a different drawing with each contest – the head of a woman with a feather in her hat, an Indian with full headdress, a kitten playing with a ball of yarn, or bird's nest nestled on a tree branch. But Flora Ann never seemed to be selected, although she kept sending in her money for the entrance fee. It was after several attempts she joined the Peace Corps.

Flora Ann requested to be cremated and to rest for all eternity in one of her clay pots…one of the few she made with a lid.

Obituary for Fay Preggers Agent

Friends and family of Fay Preggers Agent, age 74, would like to pay their respects at this sad time. "Mama Fay", as she was called, was the mother of twelve children and the grandmother of too many to count. Born in Bunkum, Maine, she lived in the small rural community of Bluffton, just outside of Bunkum until her death. While attending Bunkum High School, "Mama Fay" was in the Future Homemakers Club and Knitting Club. Her Senior picture described her as "out sick a lot" and saying, "I must have missed that period" because she was allowed many early morning bathroom passes. Fellow students remembered her crying in Home Economics many times and that she was excused from gym class quite a bit.

Once at a rival high school's area spring track meet, students from Bunkum overheard the opposing team cruelly taunt her by saying, "Nothin' says lovin' like somethin' in the oven." She was voted "Cutest Couple" Senior Superlative by the 1964 Bunkum Senior Class. "Mama Fay" was married three times. Her first marriage to "Skinny" Darrell Blacksheep was held the day after high school graduation. Six days after graduation her family immediately grew with the first of her twelve children. They named their baby Barbara Blacksheep. Darrell was not cut out for marriage and skedaddled leaving "Mama Fay" just after their twins were born one year later. The twins survived only six days. It was a sad time for "Mama Fay."

Then she met her second husband, William DeLyte. She and William had another set of twins, Joy Anna DeLyte and Afternoon DeLyte. William was pleased when they finally had the son, Fuller DeLyte, who he had always longed for. William was in the military and was stationed overseas for a year without a home visit. A daughter was born during his overseas assignment. "It's a miracle!" Mama Fay said at the time and named the baby Angel DeLyte. William divorced "Mama Fay" shortly after receiving the news.

This left "Mama Fay" with five children and no husband. Rich, old Mr. Agent, age 76 at the time of his proposal and the wealthiest land baron in Expectant, Maine, offered his hand in marriage to "Mama Fay" and her brood. Stillborn triplets arrived the next year, but in their five years of marriage before Mr. Agent's death, four more children arrived, IMA Agent, EFBEI Agent, Secret Agent, and Undercover Agent. "Mama Fay" inherited her husband's millions.

May we pay our respect to "Mama Fay" and her

family.

Obituary for Della Ware

Miss Della Ware, a retired Bunkum High School English teacher died of natural causes September 2018. Date of death is undetermined as Miss Ware lived alone except with her 6 cats.

Neighbors noticed Miss Ware sitting an unusually long time on her metal porch swing without moving while the swing, run by battery, continued to swing in the breeze. After two days of seeing her in the same position and with no cats to be seen in her yard, friends became suspicious and called the police. First responders came to the scene with police and found her dead of cat-scratch-fever.

Della Ware loved literature. While teaching at Bunkum High School in the 1950s, 1960s, and 1970s before her retirement, she often had her students write compare and contrast papers regarding literature. Becoming infatuated with John F. Kennedy in the late 50s and early 60s, students remembered that she would ask them to compare or contrast a piece of literature with JFK- the Senator, later the President, and still later the assassinated President. One student (who asked to remain anonymous) remembers a paper topic that she was assigned to write in which she was to compare *The Scarlet Letter* with Marilyn Monroe's involvement with the president. Another student was assigned comparing the lifestyle of the 1920s *Great Gatsby* with JFK's behaviors as a young college student and young senator.

Miss Ware sponsored the Debate Team called "Arguably The Best". After Kennedy's assassination, she mostly had her students debate the theories of the assassination such as the 1) New Orleans conspiracy 2) CIA conspiracy 3) Secret Service conspiracy 4)

Cuban government conspiracy 5) Lyndon Johnson's conspiracy, 5) The Mafia's conspiracy, and so on…There was plenty of material for debate.

Her home library was full of literature books, which boasted many first editions in her collections, but especially interesting was her collection of sensational banned books which she also collected. And to no one's surprise, she had her own private JFK Library section containing every title ever written about the president.

Also found among her belongings were her English class lessons plans over the course of her 37 years of teaching. In those plans were notes she never delivered to students which some read, "Dear Earl E. Byrd, Good Luck in your coming years. Remember, high school graduation is not the end but the beginning of a new adventure…but not until you turn in that make-up composition."   "Dear Phil Landerer, Good Luck in your coming years. Remember, high school is not the end but only the beginning of a new adventure…but not until you finish taking that Senior exam so I may grade it before I fill out your grade on your report card by tomorrow when grades are due." And " Dear Eva Destruction, Good Luck in your coming years. Remember, high school is not the end but only the beginning of a new adventure…but not until your return that school library book checked out in my name that you used for your John Fitzgerald Kennedy comparison paper of Walt Whitman's "O Captain, My Captain."

Whether these students ever received a copy we do not know.

Della Ware donated her body to science. Her will stated she wanted to make sure there were no conspiracy theories surrounding her demise as she became more delusional - especially regarding the government over time. She told many that she knew, *they* knew, she was a "keeper" of sensitive information and an expert in the biographical and historical information on the former president.

For those who have expressed interest in adopting one or more of Miss Ware's kitties, good luck with that. Having been in the home without food or water while Miss Ware's remains were still swinging on the front porch, when the Department of Animal Control came to collect the felines they saw her entire JFK library section (and only that section) was shredded to pieces by the cats being cooped up for days and they escaped without ever being caught.

Obit for Morris Kode

Morris Kode, all – county, all – region, all – state basketball player from Bunkum High School out of Bunkum, Maine was found unconscious in his home on Court Lane last week.

Morris Kode, age 73, and 6' 9" in height, 233 lbs. in weight at the top of his playing career, was well known throughout the northeastern United States while playing for the Holy Toledo University Basketball Team in Toledo, Ohio. He was Michael Jordan before there was Michael Jordan.

While at Bunkum High, he made basketball exciting from tip-off to the last sound of the buzzer. His top score for most points in one game was against archrival, St. Vincent. Beating the St. Vincent Vampires 139 to 27, Kode's contribution was 115 points. No matter how many times the Vampires tried to trip, throw the ball over Kode's head, or just plain aim and shooting the ball at his genitalia, nothing seemed to stop Morris Kode. "He must wear some thick, super-improved, specially made jockstrap," said the St. Vincent's coach.

While playing for Holy Toledo Tornadoes, Morris never forgot his roots back in Bunkum. Fondly thinking about where he came from he would say, "I am just playing this simple kid's game that I loved back at Bunkum Middle and High School but here I am making more money than the President of the United States."

Kode was an excellent outside shooter but a poor ball handler. Fans never fell asleep at his games, because they were afraid they might get hit by a pass. It happened a lot. And it didn't help getting the ball in the hands of another outside shooter on the team.

Tornado Coach B. B. Gunn said once, "We have a great bunch of outside shooters. Unfortunately, all our games are played indoors."

Fans sitting behind the players bench remember overhearing the Toledo coach during one tense game when Kode was benched because of reaching the foul limit say to him, "Kode, the score is tied and there is ten seconds left in the game. What would you do?"

Kode answered, "I'd scoot on down the bench to see better."

During his years at Toledo, several new official referee signals were created.

1. Another referee signal used during the game was *No Public Display of Affection in the Stands.*
2. Another ruling was *No Visiting Team Wallets Stolen from Visiting Locker Room.*
3. A third ruling demanded there would be *Time Out to Pump the Ball.*
4. There would be *No Legal Use of the Ten-Foot Gym Ceiling to Help Make Shots to the Basket.*
5. This signal was definitely needed for a long time – *Penalty For Any Team's Fan for Starting a Fight in the Parking Lot.*
6. And last and more important, *Time Out to Air Out the Gym.*

Taken to <u>We Did Our Best Hospital</u>, doctors were unable to revive Morris Kode.

Services to be announced after a special coffin is made to lay Mr. Kode rest, which may take a while. Check back with Coffins So Nice, You'll Wanna Die Twice Funeral Home for burial arrangements.

Obituary for Sharon Sharealike

Sad news out of Bunkum, Maine this week. Sharon Sharealike, age 70, was pronounced dead at Discount Doctor's Hospital. Graduating from Bunkum High School in 1964, people were just amazed at her age, thinking she must still be in her early 50's. She had good reason to look years younger, her father was a dermatologist who never let Sharon and her brother see the light of day, even going so far as to taking them in the summers to the community pool thirty minutes before its nightly closing at 8:00 p.m. There were no friends left to neither play nor swim with, so Sharon remained a very isolated child.

Growing up she had to find indoor pursuits such as crocheting hot pad patterns, baby-sitting blind children, taking tuba lessons, and paint by numbers art. She grew into a gorgeous five foot ten inch brunette bombshell, and with her blue eyes and that gorgeous skin tone, she was asked by Menken's Department Store to be a "live" mannequin and roam the women's department wearing designer fashions. Even with the faux pas that happened in her first year of modeling as a Menken's Mannequin (of which her arrest record was expunged), she was then promoted to the Marciszewski, Maine store as a floating mannequin for that location. Later, she became a runway model for the Lewiston Department Store fashion show luncheons.

At Bunkum High School she was in the Tuba Club who toot-tooted anywhere they were asked in Bunkum to toot. They tooted yearly for the Supporters of the Bunkum Landfill Fall Dance and she was the Chairman for the Bunkum High School's Janitors' retirement fund.

She recently had moved back to Bunkum to look after her younger brother. She started writing poetry in her advanced age. Her brother plans to read her most famous limerick at her funeral, entitled, "Ode to The Aging Porcelain Doll."

Even when I take a nap,
I wake up and feel like crap,
Eyesight going, too.
What's a girl to do?
When she sees her arm-fat flap?

Obituary for Tommie Ann Dickerson Ball

Our beloved, Tommie Ann Dickerson Ball, passed away on August 20, 2018. Known to all as Tommie Ann Dickerson Ball, she lived in or near Bunkum, Maine all her life, even the years she attended Bunkum Junior College from 1964-1966. She married fellow Bunkum High School student, Hyman "Hy" Ball. They had one daughter, Cricket Ball.

While at Bunkum High, Tommie Ann was the official school mascot, the Jesters. She was a member of the Jester-Rooters – 1,2,3.4; Pep Club 1,2,3,4; She was Sophomore Class Vice-President – 2; She was the Student Council's Sergeant-At-Arms 3,4; the newspaper staff – 1,2; the yearbook staff – 3,4; YMCA Women's group Orphans Meet and Greet; Bunkum-Villianeens 1,3,4; Young Men's and Mom's Valentine Soiree Dance Ticket sales and decorations 3; faculty lounge usherette – 1,2,3,4; Key Club's 6th runner-up Sweetheart Competition; Junior Varsity Golf Whisperette Rooters – 1, Captain – 2.

Her yearbook Senior Picture commented that she was known for being pert, sweet, and peppy. Friends said that in high school her bedroom was full of stuffed court jesters and Bobby Sherman posters. She wore madras plaid almost every day -unless it was a game day, when she wore the Court Jester mascot outfit. She was such a dedicated mascot, she wore the costume no matter if it was raining or during unusually hot days. Girlfriends remember her pet peeve: cleaning her bedroom. She also loved the Beatles and Ringo Starr was her favorite.

She was known for saying, "Mind your own beeswax!" "That's great!" "Neat!" and "Let's not spoil it."

While at Bunkum Junior College, she obtained an Excellent in Typing certificate and since no one could replace her enthusiasm as the Bunkum Court Jester mascot, she continued to bring her happy disposition as the high school mascot for two more years after high school graduation. She would drive back home one and a ½ hours from her junior college to entertain the fans at the games with her Jester jumps, pounces, cartwheels, and hops. The crowds would always go wild. Finally, a new "Jester" was found to replace Tommie Ann.

After obtaining her certificate, she was hired by the Bunkum School Board as a secretary for Bunkum Junior High School.

With her contagious laugh and her still bouncy steps, she will be missed all around Bunkum.

Obituary for Dale Lee Bread

Friends and family of Dale Lee Bread wish to announce his passing. Dale Lee Bread graduated in 1964 from Bunkum High School in Bunkum, Maine before moving to California for his career in entertainment.

In high school, he was a member of the trombone club, called The Funny Boners. They were a service organization who gave three free concerts every year at the Memory Loss Manor Assisted Living Home. During his Junior year, The Funny Boners jumped in to save the Junior Class Musical, *West Side Story*, where they played all the music for this play. They saved the day for the Junior Class because the entire musical theater band caught the flu. It was a triumph for this all-trombone band because they received a standing ovation for the song, "America."

Since he was first chair in the "Boners", he was Grand Marshall for Bunkum's 1964 Musical Festival, *The Music Man*, because of its famous song, "Seventy-Six Trombones".

Also while at Bunkum High, Dale Lee honed his acting chops in the drama club, From Page To Stage. He portrayed several parts in productions such as the house servant (non-speaking part) in the Senior Class production, *Caesar*; the house servant (non-speaking part) in *Dr. Jekyll and Mr. Hyde*; and in a dual role – the house servant *and* the letter carrier (both non-speaking roles) in *Romeo and Juliet*. He finally made his big break as the lead in *Frankenstein* (a non-speaking part until right before the final curtain when the monster gurgles, "Arrrgggh".)

Feeling typecast, he left for Cali to pursue his dreams of speaking roles in television or film. He joined the improv group, Drama Queens, and worked mostly behind the scenes designing and sewing costumes for their production.

His lucky break came when a television scout visited the theatre to see a production, met Dale Lee, interviewed him, found out his talent in his high school trombone group, and offered him a job on the spot. Without hesitation, he took the offer right away.

The job was with CBS and they offered Mr. Bread a lifetime job with all the Charlie Brown seasonal television productions. After signing his contract and feeling he had made it to the big leagues, he soon found out his role was again another non-speaking part as the trombone-voiced-teacher, Miss Othmar. He wah-wahed until his untimely death at the age of ninety-five. Learning of Dale Lee Bread's passing, a CBS spokesperson gave this press release, "With this recent death information, Mr. Bread has yet to be replaced on the Charlie Brown series but will never be replaced in our hearts. You're a good man, Dale Lee Bread. Rest in peace. Wah, Wah."

Obituary for Alma Geddon

This just in: Bunkum, Maine – Bunkum High School former Girls Physical Education teacher, Alma Geddon, passed away today from being hit with a bowling ball while watching her teammates from Almost Heaven Nursing Home bowl in the *Over 90 League*. Her wheelchair was placed too close to her teammate's throwing arm and while the player was lining up her roll, she swung back too far (unbelievably) and Ms. Geddon was accidently hit in the head causing her death.

"Such a shame, too," her suitemate at the nursing home was quoted saying to the Bunkum Police investigating the incident. Continuing, "She was, 'Manager! Get that fly away from me!' such an interesting person who 'Shoo! Fly! Manager?' loved all sports because 'Dag Nab It! Slap the shit out of that nasty fly and kill it,' of her position on Almost Heaven's Bowling Team. Today was her highest score *ever* and she was up next to bowl to increase her own score. Of course, just like *Depends*, we do use bumper *pads* in the gutters.

While being questioned by the police officers, other members of her bowling team had this to say about Alma -

Phyllis Stein commented, "It rained yesterday and someone took the last piece of the chocolate cake when the dog rolled over in the dirt after seeing Mel Gibson in the last movie without clothes on for the Fourth of July parade knowing that there were only four place settings at the dining room table with the baby sitting in wet diapers all day in his crib while the music was so inviting to dance to I just got up and…"

This is when the officer gets up and leaves when he realizes that comment isn't going anywhere.

Ed Settera said, "Alma Geddon? Who dat?"

Emy Nems mentioned, "Fredericka has gone to join our Lord and Savior."

An officer then says, "Not Fredericka, but Alma. Alma Geddon."

"Not Fredericka? Alma? Oh, her? She's a bitch!. Hope she goes to HELL. I can't tell you how many times she got on my last nerve. Why I remember when…" Again, another officer gets up and leaves when he realizes that comments aren't going anywhere.

After teaching physical education to all the girls at Bunkum High, Ms. Geddon coached the school's bowling team, was advisor of the Senior Class Cafeteria Tattle Tell Club, Junior Class Parking Lot Patrol and Citation Club, Sophomore Class No Bullying or PDA in the Hall Monitors Club, and Freshman Class Keep-it-Quiet in the Library Club.

She was 5th runner-up 1959 Teacher of the Year, 4th runner-up 1960 Teacher of the Year, and 3rd runner-up 1961, 1962, 1963, 1964 Teacher of the Year. When 1965 nominations were held and her name was thrown in the hat once again, she told the faculty to "just go f****! themselves" and removed her name from ever being in contention of that honor again.

She retired after thirty-seven years teaching and bowled every Tuesday and Thursdays at Can't Believe It's Not Gutter Bowling Alley until she joined the Bowl Movements when she moved into Almost Heaven Nursing Home.

Services to be announced at a later date.

Obituary for Betsy McCall Butterick

Mrs. Betsy McCall Butterick, age 86, passed on November 15, 2018 at the home of her daughter in Bunkum, Maine. A home economics teacher at Bunkum High School for 30 years, Mrs. Butterick always said that teaching young girls about how to make a beautiful home, sew beautiful clothes, and create delicious meals was her destiny.

Because she was the granddaughter of McCall's magazine's 1873 founding publisher, James McCall, Betsy knew her name alone was identifiable. In 1951, the magazine concocted and promoted a paper doll by the name of Betsy McCall with cutout clothes that was printed in most issues.

Mrs. McCall Butterick graduated from the Coast Guard Institute of Technology with a degree in fashion design. She later studied at the Cordon Bleu Cafeteria School of Food Preparation. With fashion and food training, she added a Sewing Certificate from the Butterick's Women's Dress Pattern Industry of Tissue Paper Dress Patterns. With this well-rounded degree, she began teaching at Bunkum High School.

While studying at Butterick, she met and married the grandson of its founder, Buddy Butterick. They had one daughter, Simplicity.

While at Bunkum, Mrs. Butterick was advisor of the Future Housewives of America because she said, "Homemaking is the oldest profession in the world. Our Future Housewives of America members' intention is to make a lifetime career out of it."

The club's activities included annual trips to Bunkum's Pick and Save Grocery where her students learned how to shop for nutritional foods on a mediocre budget. Mrs. Butterick said, "This is a necessity for young wives and is a science just like astrophysics."

Also while at Bunkum High, Betsy McCall Butterick was advisor for the Mopping Club, Ironing Club, Dusting Club, Sweeping Club, Sewing Club, and Cooking Club. She was the sponsor of the Homemade Soup Bone Sale Fundraiser for Homeless Animals.

The Sewing Club pitched in to sew headscarves for their fundraiser, Homebound Housewives Without Cars. These colorful scarves were wide enough to cover most hair rollers and curlers should the housewives share a vehicle to transport them out for a day of shopping and so that they wouldn't have to take down their curlers and style their hair before their husbands came home from work that evening.

After retirement, she traveled to visit family in Louisville, Kentucky. While there, she was drawn to a garlic cheese grits recipe served at a Kentucky Derby party. Never having grits before, she investigated this new phenomenon for this Maine girl and came back up north and started writing a cookbook entitled, The Giddy Up! Kentucky Derby Grits Recipes and More.

Her recipes read like a Forrest Gump Shrimp Cook Book: Old Fashioned Creamy Grits, Cheesy Southern Grits, Cheesy Shrimp and Grits, Creamy Stone Ground Grits, Mexicorn Grits, Southwestern Grits, Heirloom Red Corn Grits, Shrimp and Grits, Tomato Cheese Grits, Pimento Cheese Grits, Amish Grits Casserole, Bacon Shrimp and Cheddar Grits, Shrimp and Cheddar Grits with Collard Greens, Yankee Grits, Sea Island Shrimp and Grits, Buffalo Shrimp and Blue Cheese Grits, Cajun Garlic Shrimp and

Grits, Grits with Corn and Onion Greens, Uncle Pooh's Shrimp, Sausage, and Grits, Creamy Goat Cheese Grits, Garlic Basil Shrimp and Grits, Carolina Brunch-Style Grits, and Ham and White Cheddar Grits, just to name a few. Her book reached as high as #4 on Amazon in the category: Yankee Tries Grits, Likes Them, and Writes a Recipe Book.

Obituary for Frank N. Beans

Funeral for Frank N. Beans was held at Weiner's Chapel in Bunkum, Maine. Interment was held Frankfurter Cemetery, in Manchester, England. Mr. Beans was buried beside his wife of thirty-four years, Edamame, who passed away in 1998 from hemagglutinin. Frank met Edamame, while both were working for the Heinz Corporation in Kitt Green, suburb of Wigan, in Greater Manchester, England.

While Frank worked in-house in advertising for the company, Edamame worked in production as a taste tester. Hemagglutinin is another name for food poisoning caused from eating soaked raw or undercooked beans. Heinz Baked Beans are produced by sealing raw beans and sauce in the cans, which are then placed in large pressure cookers where this production gives the sauce its thick consistency and ensures a long shelf life for the product.

In 1998, it seems Edamame got hold of a bad batch.

While at Heinz, he co-created and launched the Heinz advertising campaign slogan just three years after his 1964 high school graduation – "Nothing goes better with Weenies than Beanies." After adding a dollop of mayonnaise to a beanie weenies bowl, he also created the slogan "Frosted Dogs in a Bean Pond."

This advertising campaign won him an OBIE award, not to be confused with the Obie, an Off-Broadway award. This award is only given to those making bean commercials. It is an acronym for Only Beans In Entry. Other competitors were Van Camp and Bush advertising.

Frank N. Beans loved being in the creative department. To promote kids to take notice of their product, they held a yearly contest in Manchester just for them: Sneeze a Beanie Weenie Through Your Nose Contest. The child that sneezed the weenie the farthest won a year's supply of Heinz Beans.

After retirement he moved back to Bunkum, Maine, to be close to his twin sister, Chili, who was having trouble with her kidneys. But his fame followed him and Bunkum gave him a hero's welcome by conducting a parade in his honor. Oscar Mayer loaned the Weiner-Mobile just for the occasion (well, their weenies *are* in Heinz Beanie Weenies…)

His children, Cheryl (who they nicknamed, Chick Pea), his shortest child, Ben (who went by the name Bean Sprout), Steven (called Snap Beans), and his tallest child, Fava (who they called Pole) chose to live in Kitt Green with their own families. They travel back and forth to the United States every year.

While at Bunkum High School, Frank was in the Audio-Visual Aid club known as the "Flicker Fellows." Besides helping with the setting up the reel-to-reel projectors for in-class educational films for Hygiene lessons, Driver's Ed lessons, Family Living lessons, and Boys' Physical Education Classes, they also plugged in the school extension cords and adjusted the Principal's microphone during assemblies.

Obituary for Pete Moss

Mr. Pete Moss, 97 years old, from Bunkum, Maine, passed away from – unknown causes– Friday, April 13th, 2018. It was an unlucky day for him and his extended family. Everything that could have gone wrong did that day.

Mr. Moss was admitted to the emergency room with breathing difficulties early on the morning of Friday the 13th. After receiving breathing treatments, he was sent back home to recuperate. But because of an unexpected and quick cold front for April, an unforeseen snowstorm amassed in Bunkum in the late afternoon. Even meteorologists could not have predicted the amount of snow dumped on Bunkum. Because of this event, the roads were impassible and when Mr. Moss started experiencing problems again, his family was unable to get him to the emergency room before his demise.

Mr. Moss taught mathematics at Bunkum High School for 39 years. He received his B.S. from Liberty University. While at Bunkum, he was the sponsor of the Slide-Rule Club, known as the "*Slip Sticks.*" The club met on Thursdays to learn more about the history, lore, and many handy uses of the slide rule. The members competed with slide-rule clubs from other schools in contests or arithmetic skill and in 1964, Mr. Moss was proud of his protégé, Matt Tress, who placed third in the State Divide-Off.

Mr. Moss was also the advisor for the *Square Rooters* who sponsored the annual Mix 'n Math dinner dance for many years and was in charge of the slide-rule tie clip fundraiser for orphans.

Divorced, he left behind his beloved Pharaoh hound, Abacas.

Obituary for Gianni Farrari

It is with sadness the family of Gianni Xavier Farrari, age 76, announces his passing in Bunkum, Maine.

Gianni, or Johnny as most of his friends called him, attended Bunkum High School graduating in 1968. He was well liked by his classmates and many of his friends fondly remember him for his sayings which included, but were not limited to, "Do unto others before they do unto you", "You wish", "I was only resting my eyes" and "I'll get down on my knees if you'll get down on your elbows!"

He was a popular student even if he was not a studious one. He was known to pull some real boners while he maintained his record as pocket pool champ at Dominic's Pool Hall on 9th Avenue in Bunkum. Johnny held the record for two decades. Besides his main squeeze, Anna Sofia Martini, Johnny loved his 1958 Mercury turnpike cruiser. Every Sunday after church services at the Sacred Heart of Villa Messina at the corner of 3rd Street and DeRosa, Johnny would wash and wax his car with Anna Sofia in attendance. Mrs. Farrari would make her special lasagna for her entire family and Anna Sofia.

Johnny was the oldest of 10 sisters, including *but not limited to*, Andrea Doria Farrari, Luce Morales Farrari, Faye Slift Farrari, Carmen Ghis Farrari, Tania Hyde Farrari, Dell Monte Farrari, Sadie Word Farrari, Stella Constellation Farrari, Val Vita Farrari, and Lotta Zitts Farrari. Johnny's father seemed to have disappeared before Lotta Zitts was born.

Starting high school in 1960 with all his friends from elementary and junior high school, Johnny's interest in school seemed to nose dive as he progressed through high school. Although winner of the annual Freshman-Sophomore Fall Sock-Hop Dance Contest while he was a Freshman in 1960 and again as a Sophomore in 1962, Johnny's seemed to find girls more interesting than school. After breaking it off with Anna Sofia Martini after his sophomore year, he seemed to enjoy his freedom as he said, "Why make one girl miserable when you can make so many happy?" He was a member of the Hot Rod Club his Freshman year, both Sophomore years, all three Junior years, and lastly twice his Senior year, graduating in 1968.

After graduation in 1968, he was hired as a mechanic at Al Patrino's Garage. Soon after in December 1968, Anna Sofia Martini re-entered the picture and they were married in August 1969, with their twins Andrea and Elena, who were born September 1969 to join their family. He and Anna Sofia divorced in October 1969. Johnny never remarried. He will be interred at the Holy Sacred Hearts Cemetery, Italian section, to rest for all eternity.

Obituary for Gilbert O'Sullivan

This obituary comes out of the Bunkum newspaper, *The Bunkum News*. Gilbert Sullivan O'Sullivan passed away Monday, July 22, 2018. Mr. O'Sullivan is survived by his wife of 51 years, Maureen, and their three children, Rhonda Campfire O'Sullivan, Eva Dustruction O'Sullivan, and Monty Zuma O'Sullivan. He was 72 years old and a life-long resident of Bunkum.

During his four years at Bunkum High School, where he graduated as the class of 1964's Salutatorian, he was on the Honor Roll 1,2,3,4; Winner of TIME Magazine's Current Events Contest; State Science Fair Honorable Mention; Chess Club 2,3; Stamp Club 1,2; Marvelous Math Mad Men 1,2,3,4; Radio Club 3,4; Paraboleers 1,3,4; Insect Club 2; Reptile Club 2; Spider Club 1,3; Rocketry Club 1.2.3.4; with his Grade Average 99.9997 he was awarded a full four year scholarship to the United States War College graduating in 1968. His yearbook described him as being big on trig, always prepared, and continually wearing a slide-rule tie clip with mismatched socks. He was studious and even took notes at lunch. He was eager in the classroom and his classmates remember him by his always saying, "Me, sir! Pick me! I know!" He was known to even study *in* study hall.

While at the U.S. War College, he was a member of Sigma Sigma Pi – academic Entomology Club; Kudos for Cadets, water boy for the War College's female field hockey team; and student leader for his Junior Class…no wait, that's student leader for his Junior Class dorm…no, for his dorm's hall. Meeting his future wife while she was on the college hockey team, they married their Senior year and lived in Student Housing on campus. After college, the two moved back to Bunkum to begin their married life together while Mr. O'Sullivan became the owner of O'Sullivan Electronics for the last 50 years.

Obituary for Custodian
Scabrous Pronunciation

It's a sad day in Bunkum, Maine, when the news of beloved Bunkum High School Custodian, Obudgh Rmijalth, passed away before Thanksgiving Day. Mr. Rmijalth had worked for the school system for forty-five years, before finally retiring in 2004. He was popular with all the students but especially the high school students in Bunkum.

Although he knew the culprits while working at Bunkum High, he never tattled on the students, who in 1964 created much ruckus with a wave of vandalism that struck that year. Called into the office of the principal to obtain any knowledge he might have, Mr. Rmijalth pleaded ignorance, which with his IQ wasn't hard, of any information about the student crimes.

It was a terrible school year at BHS with Principal Marcus Absent trying to solve the mystery of who created the large four-letter word measuring approximately six by fourteen inches over the washbasin sinks in the downstairs boys washroom. After the Christmas holidays that year, the high school had been plagued by similar vandalisms including willfully defaced plaques, walls, waste-baskets, lockers, water fountains, behind hot radiators, bag lunches, gym shoes, mirrors, school bus gas tanks, teachers' lounge water coolers, cafeteria trays, art supply cabinets, and the new Student Council sponsored Student Suggestion Box, which Class President, Chuck Steaks, had hoped would "spur good citizenship and an opportunity to air student views and gripes. Instead, the only thing that's gotten aired out is the Student Suggestion Box," he stated.

Principal Absent stated that vandalisms "would not be tolerated, even if it means boarding up all lavatories or requiring students to attend the restrooms under a buddy system."

Asking the student body for their help of identifying the perpetrators while Mr. Rmijalth stayed mum, Principal Marcus Absent also announced the reward of 500 Good Citizenship Credits to any student for information leading to the capture and expulsion of the culprit. The Good Citizenship Credit points would then be applied to their school records to boost any student's college application.

Mr. Rmijalth remained popular with all the students for his quiet disposition and never leaking the information of who might be involved in the destruction of the school. Probably because of his faulty English skills.

Even with adding more hall monitors, Principal Absent also chastised students at the "Who is the Mad Vandal?" assembly by warning them if they didn't cooperate in helping identify this culprit, he would cut off their Eskimo Pie and chocolate milk privileges.

The Bunkum Daily News featured many stories about the school vandalism. Still, Mr. Rmijalth remained mum.

After retirement, Rmijalth could not care for himself, so friends, family, and members from his church, Russia's Orthodox Three Saints Onion Dome, chipped in to send him to At Heaven's Gate Retirement Home which he subsidized his room and board by sweeping the home for free.

He was beloved by many students because of his quiet demeanor and big toothy grin.

Obit for Sally Mander

Condolences are sent across the ocean to the family of Lmk Lzmk Luzmk, AKA Sally Mander here in the United States. Lmk, who will be known in the entirety of this article as Sally, was born in Kefauverstan and after graduation at Bunkum High School, she attended the International Studies Program in World Relations at the Junior United National College in Shreveport, Louisiana. Miss Mander passed away in August 2018, while performing a top secret mission as a Spy Sister for the United Nationals. She was flown back to her home country where she will be cremated.

Sally Mander came to Bunkum, Maine as an exchange student with the Fourth Tier Exchange Student Program sponsored by the Jiffy Lube Company. She began her studies in the seventh grade at Bunkum Junior High School and continued her study program with her host family, Mr. and Mrs. Claude Balls. She graduated in 1964 from Bunkum High School. She visited her family in Kefauverstan during the summers. The exchange program was the brainchild of Peg Board, wife of Bunkum's Jiffy Lube's owner and manager.

With all the time spent in the United States, it would seem Sally would seamlessly fit into the typical role of a teenager in Bunkum, yet some things always stood out as awkward. She still continued to comb her hair with a fork, which was a custom in her home country because forks were a rarity and thought to be better used in this fashion than used as an eating utensil. She continued to stick Kit Kat candy bars in her ears and rub Reese's Peanut Butter cups into her clothing.

She was known for saying, "Is not better to cry tears for meat taken from sacred cows with bladder stuffed elm leaves?" and "Boy bring strong ox as gift to home. We see fire across shore. Am strong. Why?"

Sally attended the 1964 Spring Senior Trip to New York's United Nations tour. While on tour, she was declared lost for two days in Manhattan but eventually safely showed up at the 1964's World's Fair's unique Unisphere where all students were supposed to meet for the bus ride back home. No one, including the chaperones, asked any questions about her whereabouts for two days as they wouldn't have been able to understand anything she said about it anyway.

She was a member of the Women's Chorus, but unable to sing the words in the songs, she just opened and closed her mouth at random times during performances. She also participated in Senior Stunt Night where students were given an exotic taste of entertainment from Sally's native land with her authentic "foot" dance on a gymnastics bar. She tied for first place after falling off the bar at the end of her routine and had to be transported by ambulance to the hospital.

Sally was last seen at graduation from Junior United National American College in Shreveport, Louisiana until her demise. She never spoke about her job because she was never seen again until she showed up as a Jane Doe in Bunkum Hospital. It was later determined to be Sally Mander, age 83. Her death certificate has no cause of death on it.

Friends and family from high school will always remember Sally's broad smile with her lack of teeth looking like the final four of college basketball's

March Madness. While in college, she quit opening
her mouth to smile and just began to grin.

    Friends wish to say to Sally's family, "Hold on.
Big ox finds shore and brings wretched refuse,"
which was one of Sally's favorite sayings.

Obituary for Nun, Ann Arbor

Miss Ann Arbor, age 72, passed away Halloween night from a frightful scare of seeing the Devil, or so she thought. Miss Arbor, a former nun at the Downtown Abbey, not to be confused with "Downton Abby"—the English television drama, was always deathly scared of the Devil from her Catholic scripture. On October 31st, children and their teachers paraded in costume from nearby Bunkum Elementary School in Bunkum, Maine, to her nursing home, Geezer Glen, so as to entertain the inhabitants. Miss Arbor had a front row rocking chair seat and after the parade route turned the corner from the school and headed in the direction of the living facility, the aides from Geezer Glen noticed Ann Arbor turned pale and collapsed.

It appears that one of the teachers in the group, in the spirit of the Halloween revelry with his students, dressed up as one of the New Jersey Devils, professional hockey player. His charade was so real that it frightened Sister Ann and she went into cardiac arrest. Her last words were, "Coach Brock, I missed last period!" which no one understood what that was supposed to mean except for a few of her peers from high school who now lived with her at the assisted living. Wanting to chuckle, they held their giggles because of the dire situation. She was taken back to Downtown Abbey for burial along with other sisters and mothers who preceded her in their personal cemetery, Hope Eternal Cemetery.

Sister Ann attended Bunkum High School in Bunkum, Maine, graduating in 1964. She was a very popular (*very popular*) student. She was the Sweetheart for the 9th grade all boys service club, The

Bachelors. In 10th grade she served as Sweetheart for another service club, The Randy Dandys. When she was in the eleventh grade, she was elected Sweetheart for two organizations, The Cad Abouts and the Bunkum High School football team. Although voted "Most Popular" her senior year, Ann Arbor, was never elected Sweetheart again as she seemed to disassociate from anything to do with typical high school pursuits. She joined the Bunkum City Theatre Group, Break A Leg, for their 1964 Spring production of *The Flying Nun,* where she played the lead role of all the nuns. The play was performed for the Easter Season in Bunkum.

After graduation, Ann Arbor, took her vows to become a convent nun and it was there she remained the rest of her days in Downtown Abbey. Her parents and 13 siblings were so proud of her being so popular in high school and then for her selfless career choice after high school.

More news to follow.

Obituary for Esther Darke

Funeral arrangements for Esther Echols Darke were held at Burns Funeral Home and Crematory in Bunkum, Maine, Saturday, August 11, 2018. Esther, known to all as Essie, graduated from Bunkum High School in 1964. Her husband, Alfredo D. Darke, passed away in 1998, after thirty years of marriage.

Before her marriage to Alfredo, it was common knowledge to all that for many years, Essie had a huge high school crush on Terry Cloth. It was so well known by her classmates as she tried to secure at least one date with Terry all during her high school years with their help. According to many, Terry avoided her for four years until she finally got her wish to be his Senior prom date. This took place only because of his last minute disappointment from his original prom date. One of his proposed date's girlfriends called Terry to cancel for her friend because she had to wash her hair that evening and couldn't attend the prom with him after all. Wondering what to do now that he had purchased his tux and her corsage, he asked Essie at the last minute and she was thrilled beyond thrills, even though he picked her up for the prom after it had already started.

She told girlfriends she "felt it in her bones that Terry would eventually ask her to the dance and not one of the most popular cheerleaders at Bunkum High as she heard he might ask to go with him." They remembered her saying, "He doesn't stand a chance getting a date with her and will realize after tonight that I am the girl of his dreams." Little did she know the cause of her invitation.

It was a dream come true for Essie. After prom but before graduation, she wrote in his yearbook, "Dear

Terry, What a swell guy you are. I really mean that, because you are a swell guy. It's been swell to be in your classes these past four years. I know we will have a great future together after graduation, so don't lose touch. I'll never forget sitting only four desks apart from each other in English, History, and Chemistry. I tried really hard to get in your Chemistry lab group but somehow my name was misspelled and instead of Echols it was Rechols and I was too far down on the list to be assigned alphabetically to your group. I don't know how that happened. Your best buddy was in charge of grouping the entire class for lab time. Oh, well, we still walked in the halls to lunch together alphabetically and we were just three people apart then. But it seems you always ended up sitting in the last seat of the row at the table when our teacher reprimanded us for misbehaving and made us sit alphabetically in the lunchroom, too.

Remember the time that we both came to the same Open House our Senior year? I'll never forget that. And I'll never forget when you asked me to go to prom and I had to rush to get my dress ready by 9 o'clock. We had some really great times there, even when I couldn't find you for about an hour and a half and all your friends said you were sick in the boys' bathroom. It was OK that you had to take me home early because you had all that homework you had to do.

I've kept my baby's breath corsage in my high school scrapbook along with our prom picture. Someone told me you cut out my half of the picture from your photograph of us but I don't believe it because we had such a swell time, as you said over and over when I asked you all evening if you were having fun."

According to friends, Essie's heart was broken when she never heard from Terry again over the summer before he left for college out of state. She mourned for three years until she met Alfredo D. Darke whom she met at her church outside of the Bunkum city limits. He never knew that he came in second in Essie's heart but resembling Terry Cloth somewhat in looks and fearing she would be an old maid, she accepted his marriage proposal and within a year they married. They had no children.

Obituary for Collie Raddo

With sadness, Bunkum Funeral Home announces the passing of Miss Collie Raddo, age 88, of Bunkum, Maine. Miss Raddo never married. Miss Raddo attended Canal Zone Junior College and graduated with a Bachelor of Arts in Romance Languages from Chihuahua State College. She taught Spanish in the Bunkum City School System and spent her entire 37 years at Bunkum High School until her retirement. While at Bunkum, she was the advisor of *Pinatas y Sombreros* and *Future Stewardesses* clubs. *Future Stewardesses* later changed their name to *Future Flight Attendants Club* and allowed boys to participate. Miss Raddo promoted having young men participate in her sponsored club, so it was exciting when finally the all-male Bunkum School Board voted unanimously for males to join. Miss Raddo was a life-long member of the *Mile-High-Club*.

The *Pinatas y Sombreros Club* annually held their "Poke at Pinatas" Meet and Greet for Underprivileged Children in the Bunkum area. It was held at the YMCA on 4th Street where Miss Raddo volunteered her time as a tutor to teach Spanish to high school students (mostly boys), and to teach English as a second language to Spanish speaking students (again, mostly boys).

While the sponsor of the *Future Stewardesses Club*, she taught young girls about the perks of being a stewardess as a career path. These gals were on their way up in the world. They met every Thursday evening to practice friendly grins and balancing trays. The "*Flighties*" held an annual "Coffee, Tea, or Milk" for members of other clubs in the school. Every year they led Bunkum's ever popular *Jester Safety Society*,

"Seat Belts On, and No Smoking in the Student Parking Lot."

The 1964 club's flight captain (when the young men became involved it switched to president), Claire Voyance who still lives in the Bunkum area, commented that Miss Raddo had a great influence on her as a student and a club member. She mentioned she didn't know which foreign language to take while in high school and it was because of *Future Stewardesses* that she finally settled on Spanish and became an international flight attendant because of her strong Spanish-language skills.

Miss Raddo never won any teaching awards although she was very well liked by her students, especially her male students, and was well thought of by the county school board while there were only all-male members. She was asked to be a speaker at their monthly board meetings many times.

Collie Raddo leaves behind her three kitties, Puta, Putana, and Furcia. Condolences may be sent to the mortuary which will make sure her family, still living in Chalupas, Mexico, receive these sentiments.

Connect With Me!

#1 Amazon Bestseller Business and Professional Humor

Top Four 2019 Georgia Author of the Year - Essays

Facebook: https://www.facebook.com/leestjohnauthor

Instagram: https://instagram.com/leestjohnauthor/

Website and Blog: http://www.leestjohnauthor.com/

Twitter: @LeeStJohnauthor

Newspaper: Fayette-News (Fayetteville, Ga.)

LIVE FB: HOST for "Spilling the Beans Book Club"

https://www.goodreads.com/author/show/14343509.Lee_St_John/blog

Pinterest: LeeStJohnAuthor

Guest Speaker: popular Southern humorist of observational humor

Erma Bombeck Writers Workshop

National Society of Newspaper Columnists

Atlanta Writers Club

Humorous Writers of America

Panel Member of Southern Living Magazine's THE FRONT PORCH

Can be found on Amazon.com

Acknowledgements

I would like to thank my family who puts up with me.
Bless their hearts.